Social Sciences Research

Social Sciences Research

Research, Writing, and Presentation Strategies for Students

Third Edition

Gail M. Staines

ROWMAN & LITTLEFIELD
Lanham • Boulder • New York • London

Executive Editor: Charles Harmon
Editorial Assistant: Michael Tan
Production Editor: Lara Hahn
Cover Designer: Sarah Marizan

Credits and acknowledgments of sources for material or information used with permission appear on the appropriate page within the text.

Published by Rowman & Littlefield
An imprint of The Rowman & Littlefield Publishing Group, Inc.
4501 Forbes Boulevard, Suite 200, Lanham, Maryland 20706
www.rowman.com

6 Tinworth Street, London, SE11 5AL, United Kingdom

British Library Cataloguing in Publication Information Available

Library of Congress Cataloging-in-Publication Data

Names: Staines, Gail M., 1961– author.
Title: Social sciences research : research, writing, and presentation strategies for students / Gail M. Staines.
Description: Third Edition. | Lanham : Rowman & Littlefield Publishing Group, Inc., [2019] | Revised edition of Social sciences research, 2008. | Includes bibliographical references and index.
Identifiers: LCCN 2018044286 (print) | LCCN 2018046567 (ebook) | ISBN 9781538122426 (Electronic) | ISBN 9781538122402 (cloth : alk. paper) | ISBN 9781538122419 (pbk. : alk. paper)
Subjects: LCSH: Social sciences—Research—Methodology. | Social sciences—Study and teaching (Higher)
Classification: LCC H62 (ebook) | LCC H62 .S736 2019 (print) | DDC 300.72—dc23
LC record available at https://lccn.loc.gov/2018044286

♾™ The paper used in this publication meets the minimum requirements of American National Standard for Information Sciences—Permanence of Paper for Printed Library Materials, ANSI/NISO Z39.48-1992.

Printed in the United States of America

Contents

Acknowledgments

My previous coauthors who have gone on to other things—Dr. Mark Bonacci and Dr. Katherine Johnson—have graciously allowed me to update the third edition. You have my many thanks! And to our former neighbor, Nate Smith, who had the second edition of this work assigned as required reading at college, thus inspired me to revise this work. Here's to you, Nate, for all the times you and Zach asked, "Is Staines home?"

Introduction

It has been a decade since the second edition of *Social Sciences Research* was published. Much happens in ten years. The changes to the third edition are significant in light of the way information is accessed and presented.

The original motivation to work on the first edition of this textbook, written from 1998 to 2000, came from the coauthors' experiences teaching library research and scholarly writing methods at the community college level. After a collective thirty years of college teaching experience, we found that most first-year and second-year community college students, as well as entering college and university freshmen, transfer students, and graduate students, had not received instruction in areas in which they must rapidly become proficient to excel in upper-level social sciences courses. These areas include distinguishing a scholarly source from a popular source; developing a logical, coherent, and sufficiently focused research question; conducting searches using electronic sources of information (e.g., Google Scholar, the Internet, and scholarly databases); writing papers in an acceptable format; and presenting research and projects.

We discovered that many of the finer points of these endeavors cannot be adequately treated or reviewed in writing classes covering many other topics, nor in social sciences courses already crammed full of essential material. Thus, this manual continues to be designed as a resource for students, as well as their instructors, to help students succeed in carrying out library research in the social sciences, writing formal papers in the expected format, developing a research poster for a conference, and orally presenting or defending such a paper or project.

Based on changes that have occurred since 2008 in information resources and technology, I significantly revised content on searching for information effectively, including where to search for information as well as assessing information for credibility, authority, and usefulness. In addition, I included information about how to develop a research poster and present this information at a conference or symposium.

1

Choosing an Appropriate Research Question

In high school, teachers may have assigned topics for you to research and write on. Most college courses will expect *you* to decide on a relevant topic or research question to write about. View this writing experience as an opportunity to fully use your creativity and explore your interests.

In choosing a topic to research, first remember that the topic has to hold enough interest for you personally so that you will write compellingly about it. Additionally, the topic should be of intrinsic interest to your target audience—the individuals who will be reading your research paper. You should ask yourself the following: "Is this a topic I might write a master's thesis or a doctoral dissertation on in the future?" If your answer is "yes," then this is probably a good topic to begin researching now and building upon in the future. If you are not stimulated and enthused about your research topic, you can hardly expect your readers to be.

Certain themes recur in written work over and over again. These themes can show the progress and development of thoughts and theorization. For example, if you were to read the work of a well-known researcher or author, beginning with their earliest publications and reading their subsequent works, you may find the germ of their initial ideas expressed in later writings. Often students believe that it is cheating to use the same topic for papers they write at different points in their educational careers. We believe strongly that if students are always elaborating their thoughts and doing new research on the topic to keep current in the field, then they are not plagiarizing themselves. The most interesting master's theses and doctoral dissertations are those showing that the writer's thoughts have evolved over time, most often over several years.

One important thing to remember in writing a research paper or a review of the current literature on a topic is that your personal experiences may have some tangential relevance to the topic, but may or may not be appropriate for inclusion in the final paper itself. For instance, if you are writing about physical violence in dating relationships and you have experienced this firsthand, you might insert a note to this effect in the foreword or introduction merely to explain to the reader what has prompted your interest in this subject. Or, you might use your case as an example of a certain theory after you have reviewed and written about the existing literature on this theory. It is also likely that your personal experience will not be included in the paper at all. Remember that your personal experience represents only a single case study. It may be representative of what many people in relationships have been through, but it may also be a unique pattern of events that only you have experienced. To base an entire paper on a single case study that may or may not be representative of anyone else is a non-scholarly and circular pursuit. No single case study can be considered definitive. As a researcher, the examination of a single case study would yield a very poor grade indeed.

If you select a topic of interest to you (e.g., physical violence in dating relationships), you must now modify and refine this general topic into an appropriate and workable research question. The title of your research paper should not be a categorical statement. A more scholarly and better form would be to pose a *research question* instead. Thus, rather than giving a research paper the title "The Hell Experienced by Physically Abused Women" (which is not only a categorical statement that their lives are indeed hell, but also is very general and vague), you might title your research, "Is Violence in Dating Relationships Conceptually Distinct from Violence in Marital Relationships?" Notice that this title is not only an open question, but is also focused on one specific aspect of understanding the violence in intimate relationships. This is much more feasible to research and write about than the lives of abused women, which would necessarily involve examination of economic, social, occupational, personality, and many other far-ranging issues. When you embark on a specific research question, you are attempting to answer, or to at least shed some light on, your question. Thus, when you pose the question, it should be balanced and neutral. You truly cannot know what the prior research will indicate until you have thoroughly reviewed it. Try always to formulate a research question rather than posing a categorical statement as the title of your paper. We suggest examining titles of professional scholarly journal articles to get an idea of what kinds of research questions are posed. In this way, you can get some pointers on succinctly and clearly phrasing your research question.

THE BREADTH AND DEPTH OF YOUR RESEARCH QUESTION

Your research question should be sufficiently focused so that you can effectively review the published research and treat your subject within the confines of a ten- or fifteen-page paper. Your question should not be so microscopically defined, however, that the answers to this question could not be of real interest to people in the field.

For example, the research question "Are abused women more likely to push others in supermarket lines?" is probably neither researchable nor of any real interest to even those individuals having a basic interest in these people.

You will most likely be unable to exhaustively treat whichever topic you choose, but you should pose a research question for which you can locate and review at least five published articles, as well as other sources such as books or e-books. Remember that you may not find a single article that exactly addresses your topic of interest. You may have to extrapolate from several articles—combining findings from different studies and authors, and examining the interrelationships among them—to more clearly answer your research question. Thus, you may not find a specific article on the patterns of abused women's experiences in relationships. However in several of the studies you read on this population, you might discover tangential findings or statements about abused women's patterns of behavior, even if these articles are not primarily on this topic. One word of caution is in order here: Don't overextrapolate—do not try to write an entire paper based on a few findings that are not strongly related to your topic. Paul Meehl (1960) is a theorist who stated that when extrapolating in this way, theorists must "trap" their concept of interest in a "nomothetic net." (Psychologists specifically were of primary interest to Meehl, but these concepts apply equally to other social science research endeavors.) In other words, one must be able to make sense of the relationships between the different pieces of data and explain why one feels justified in combining them and making some "leaps of logic" in subsequent conclusions.

WHICH VIEWPOINT OR DISCIPLINE WILL YOU FOCUS ON?

You must decide from which point of view to examine your research question. Will your question be mainly asked from a sociological, psychological, economic, anthropological, political, biological, or historical viewpoint? From the vantage point of which discipline will you ask your research question and focus the research? For example, a research question exploring urban decay and community-building responses to this phenomenon could be focused on each of the following ways (as well as many others, of course):

- Sociological emphasis: Are there more people living below the poverty line in U.S. urban centers?
- Psychological emphasis: Do youth growing up in decayed urban centers experience negative long-term emotional effects, or do they exhibit "resilience"?
- Economic emphasis: What has happened to the tax base in U.S. urban centers?
- Anthropological emphasis: How do U.S. urban centers compare to those of Europe?
- Political emphasis: Is there a lower rate of voter registration in U.S. urban centers?

- Biological emphasis: Is there a higher incidence of lead poisoning in urban centers, leading to lower IQ scores in school children?
- Historical emphasis: "White flight" to the suburbs: to what extent did it really occur?

As you can see, there are many different viewpoints from which to examine an issue. As a student of the social sciences, you should approach the topic from the vantage point of a specific social science; that is, anthropology and cross-cultural studies, sociology, social psychology, psychology, history, economics, criminology, political science, or geography. You might also try to understand your topic from a specific occupational focus—such as criminal justice, human services, or government—that might incorporate any of these social science perspectives. Be as focused as possible while recognizing that there is often significant overlap between disciplines.

One word of caution is in order here, especially for social work and psychology students: The fields of social work and psychology in particular frequently adopt the "medical model," and this may not be ideal for your research endeavor. What we mean by the medical model is adopting wholesale and with few modifications the terminology, techniques, and theories from one field, and using these in another field in which they may be much less appropriate and applicable.

The field of social work, especially, has relied on information used in the medical field. This is only natural if we look at the history of social work in the United States. (For instance, Mary Richmond, widely considered the "mother of social work," studied with Sigmund Freud, the "father" of psychoanalysis and a medical doctor [a neurologist] himself.) Be careful of placing too much emphasis in your research on the medical model. For example, many papers written by undergraduate students have examined questions of possible biological predispositions toward alcoholism. This can be a trap of sorts for undergraduate social work or human services students. In a nutshell, the biological research that has been done on this question has failed to explicate a particular gene or chromosome that carries the trait of alcoholism. The field is intensely focused on this question because finding such a gene or chromosome might result in some easy solution to this serious national problem. For a student studying to become a social services counselor, it would be far more interesting and useful in professional development to examine the often-neglected psychological and sociological features rather than the biological causes and effects of alcoholism. It is important to always ask yourself if the vantage point from which you are approaching a research question is the most appropriate and effective one. This will not only result in a more sensible research question, but will also facilitate your literature search.

After reading this chapter, go to Appendix C and locate Worksheet 1: Selecting a Topic and Worksheet 2: Narrowing and Focusing Your Topic. Complete both worksheets and hand these in to your professor.

2

Designing a Search for Scholarly Literature

Once you have selected a topic to research, the next step is to locate information. Searching and locating information has changed dramatically since the second edition of this book was published. This revised chapter on designing a search for scholarly literature reflects these changes in the world of information production and access.

Let's be honest. Most people (including experienced researchers) start a search for information using Google (http://www.google.com). This is neither a good nor a bad approach. It may not be the best approach, but it is a place to start. If you begin with a Google search, do not be surprised if you locate hundreds or thousands of pieces of information—some relevant to your search, and some not. A better approach would be to begin your search with Google Scholar (http://scholar.google.com). In this way, you have focused your search to research-based publications.

One of the best and most effective methods of locating the information you need is spending some time designing a search prior to actually searching for the information. Just like making a shopping list before you go shopping is effective (whether you shop online or in person), creating a research strategy enables you to make the most of your time and helps you to clearly select the information that meets your research needs. In other words, would you rather spend hours scrolling through a significant amount of irrelevant information? Or, develop a search strategy and search for information using resources that may actually have the type of information that you are looking for, in a lot less time?

This chapter provides the steps for designing a research strategy to locate information, including choosing correct keywords and selecting the most useful resources to search. The mechanics of the search itself are covered in Chapter 3. A worksheet provided in Appendix C will help you design your own research strategy for your topic.

RESEARCH STRATEGY

1. Step 1 in any search is to develop a question to research. Your question should be interesting, well defined, and narrowly delineated. Refer to Chapter 1 for suggestions on creating a research question. This is an example of a research question: "Is violence in dating relationships conceptually distinct from violence in marital relationships?"

2. Step 2 is to identify the main key words in your research question. Here are the key words from the previous example:

   violence   dating relationships   marital relationships

3. Step 3 is to develop a list of synonyms for each of the key words you identify. Using a thesaurus (online or in print) to identify possible key words is recommended. You will use these key words to search for information. Using the key words from the example, here is a list of synonyms.

violence in relationships	abuse
dating	physical abuse
marriage	abused women
women or woman	emotional abuse

4. Step 4 is to jot down the names of any scholars and experts on the topic that you are researching. You may access information not only by key words, but also by names. For example, Richard J. Gelles has written extensively on the topic of violence in the family. You could search for Gelles's name and retrieve his publications, such as journal articles and books, as well as any blog posts, websites, and other sources written by or significantly about him and his research.

5. Step 5 is to refine your topic further by indicating the time period that your research will cover. Will your paper cover research completed in the last five years? Will you focus on the past two decades? Nineteenth century? Twentieth century? Will you conduct an historical overview of the topic? Or will you do a comparative analysis of two or more decades? In the above example, you could limit your search to information from the year 2000 to the present. However, we might want to look for any major studies that have been done on this topic prior to 2000. Major studies, or what are known as *landmark studies* or *seminal studies*, provide important background information on a topic. Reading landmark studies on a topic also helps you to place your research question in a contemporary context.

6. Step 6 is to consider from what aspect or viewpoint you will approach your topic. Chapter 1 provides some insights into this. You could research your topic from the economic, legal, psychological, historical, anthropological,

political, or sociological perspectives. This example—"Is violence in dating relationships conceptually distinct from violence in marital relationships?"— could be researched from several perspectives (sociological, psychological, anthropological, etc.) depending on your own interests.

SELECTING THE MOST USEFUL RESOURCES

Again, since the second edition of this text was published, technology has exploded so that anyone can post anything on the Internet. This makes it extremely challenging to conduct a search of the literature on a specific topic. The cycle of traditional publishing does continue to exist; in traditional publishing, a researcher/author can write a book or article and submit it to a journal or a publishing company (often referred to as a publishing house) to be considered for publication.

In terms of book publishing, the researcher submits a book proposal to a potential publisher. If the publisher accepts the work (in concept), the researcher receives a contract to write the book. Before the book is published, either as an actual print book or e-book (or both), the text of the book itself is rigorously reviewed by editors and subject experts within the publishing company as well as experts in the field. Upon publication, the book is typically reviewed by subject matter experts, who publish their reviews (online and/or in print) for others to read.

Publishing in a journal follows a similar path. A researcher/author submits an article to a journal for publication. The article is typically reviewed (the reviewers are not known to the researcher, resulting in a blind review) by a number of subject matter experts; these experts comment on the work, and may recommend publishing the article without changes, publishing the article with recommended changes the author must make prior to publication, or rejecting the article for publication. If the article is rejected, a researcher may rewrite the article (or leave it as is) and submit it to another journal for publication. In the end, the article can be published in a journal (in electronic and/or print format).

In practice, some research also includes prepublications being available for reading. For example, sample chapters of a book about to be published or a draft of a journal article may be posted online, before the work is officially published. One reason this practice is taking place is to share research findings more quickly, rather than waiting for the findings to be published in the traditional manner, thus giving readers faster access to current research. However, prepublications may include errors, which will be corrected before official publication.

To make searching for information even more complex is that fact that, in addition to traditional publishing and prepublication, researchers/authors may also post information on their websites, blogs, Facebook pages, and other social media, as well as in open source electronic institutional repositories. Researchers/authors can also self-publish on such sites as Amazon. (It is important to note that anyone can claim to be an expert and self-publish their work. This is known as "vanity publishing." An author can also pay a vanity publisher to publish his or her works. In both instances, the publication is in most cases not vetted through an official publication process, leading to information that may not be accurate.) This is important to know because, when you read about searching for information later in this book, you will discover that this type of information is not always readily discoverable without searching more than Google, Google Scholar, or a library's website.

Even with new ways of publishing information, there continues to be a fairly good distinction between scholarly publications based on research, and information published for a general audience.

SCHOLARLY AND POPULAR LITERATURE: MAKING THE COMPARISON

Understanding the differences between scholarly articles and articles published in popular magazines may be a new concept to you. Whether you are giving a presentation or writing a research paper, it is preferable that you cite scholarly sources rather than information found in magazines written for a general audience. (This also holds true for postings on social media, emails, etc.) Magazines primarily serve the purpose of entertaining their audiences, and the information presented may be oversimplified or outdated. Table 2.1 is a brief guide comparing scholarly journals and popular magazines.

Table 2.1.   A Comparison of Scholarly Journals and Popular Magazines

Scholarly Journals	Popular Magazines
Bibliographies or references are included	Bibliographies or references are usually not included
Authors are experts	Authors are often generalists
Articles are signed by the author	Articles are sometimes unsigned
The audience is the scholarly reader, such as professors, researchers, and students	The audience is the general population
Standardized formats are followed, such as APA	Various formats are used
Articles are written in the jargon of the field	Articles are written for anyone to understand
Illustrations such as maps, tables, and photographs are included solely to support the text	Publications are often profusely illustrated for marketing appeal
There are few ads	There are many advertisements

Note: This table was modified from a handout created by the University of Michigan and from a figure published in "Cooperative Learning in Bibliographic Instruction," by K. N. Cook, L. R. Kunkle, and S. M. Weaver, *Research Strategies* (Winter 1995), pp. 17–25.

The Information Chain

Taking this comparative analysis one step further, it is important that you are able to identify different kinds of information sources in order to assess their credibility. One of the easiest ways to identify different kinds of information is to learn the life cycle of information or, as we refer to it here, the *information chain*. The chain of information, from idea to publication, is explained in its simplest form. Understand that there are many nuances (political and technical) that occur when information is disseminated to the public. Here, we explain the information chain in the scholarly sense.

For most researchers, the information chain begins with an idea—curiosity that leads to asking why something is the way it is. A researcher may discuss an idea or question with other experts. Discussion can take place face to face at conferences, via telephone or teleconference, via email, and other means. Due to technology, researchers can interact with each other globally. Once a researcher narrows down his or her topic to a specific research question or research statement, he or she will conduct a review of the literature. The literature is reviewed to see if someone else has already studied and answered the research question at hand. If the specific question or statement has not been studied before, or requires further research, the researcher designs and conducts a study. This can be a lengthy process involving many false starts and complications. It is not unusual for studies to be piloted, refined, and replicated to make sure results are accurate.

After this study is completed, the researcher writes an article for publication in a scholarly journal. (They may also present their research at what is known as a poster session at a professional conference.) This is how research results get disseminated. To become published in a scholarly journal is no easy task. In writing up the research results, the researcher must determine which journal is most appropriate to publish his or her article, and must obtain the journal's guidelines for publication. Each scholarly journal, such as the *Journal of Social Psychology*, has specific guidelines that potential authors must follow when submitting an article for publication. These guidelines include such items as margin width, spacing, fonts, style (e.g., American Psychological Association [APA] style), and so on. Upon submission of an article, most journals will send one copy of the article to experts in the subject field for review. Each journal has an editorial board of experts who blindly read the article, meaning that the author's name does not appear on the submitted article. In this manner, subject matter experts can review the article without bias. The experts, who intimately understand the literature in a specific field of study, review the article for content. The journal editor gathers the board's comments and returns the article to the researcher with one of the following three statements:

1. We accept your article for publication.
2. We accept your article for publication if the following changes are made . . .
3. We reject your article for publication on the basis of . . .

Usually an article will be published in a journal within eighteen months of acceptance. Research conducted by the original author is considered *primary* information. The life cycle continues as other researchers read journal articles and write books citing research that has been published in journal form. Information cited by others is considered *secondary* information, or information once removed from the original source. The original research may eventually be cited in an encyclopedia article on the topic. (Note: Wikipedia has become a known and trusted source for encyclopedia-type information, so it is acceptable to read and use this source in your work.) Generally speaking, articles in encyclopedias (online or in print) are considered *tertiary* information, meaning that it is three times removed from the original source of the research. However, sometimes authors of encyclopedia articles will cite original sources of information, too, and there are even cases in which the original researcher has actually written the encyclopedia article. If the research is considered "hot" and newsworthy, it may appear in social media and the popular press, albeit in a very condensed form. Popular magazines, such as *People* and *Time*, may publish a brief column on the topic. Television and cable news shows—such as CBS News, ABC's *Nightline*, or CNN's Headline News—may also mention the research in a short news clip. Periodically, scholarly findings are disseminated in the *New York Times*, often concurrent with publication of the information in a scholarly journal. While it can take a year or more to clear the scholarly peer review process, a "rough and ready" misinterpretation of the findings may appear suddenly in articles in the popular entertainment media. These articles may pique your interest; however, as a beginning researcher yourself, it is important to locate and read the original research article to fully understand the purpose and conclusions of the original research.

Most, if not all, research in scholarly publications goes through this chain of information to become published. The rigors of the publication process ensure that credible research gets disseminated. With the proliferation of information via the Internet, where anyone can publish anything, you must use a critical eye and read online information carefully. Some Internet sites are now peer reviewed, mirroring the traditional scholarly publication process and requiring the information to go through the same rigorous tests as information published in print or electronic journals. The best advice that we can give you is to read the information you retrieve from the Internet carefully and analyze such information for credibility by looking for bibliographies at the end of the articles and checking the credentials of the authors. (Learn about evaluating the information you find in Chapter 3.)

Take a moment after reading this chapter to turn to Appendix C and complete Worksheet 3: Scholarly versus Popular Literature; Worksheet 4: Best Places for Information, and Worksheet 5: Your Research Strategy.

3

Conducting a Search for Scholarly Literature

Once you have selected a topic to research, created your research strategy, and determined the best places to look for information, the next step is to learn the mechanics of conducting the actual search for the scholarly literature itself. This chapter provides you with some of the more effective ways to access the information you need. Much of the scholarly literature now published is available online, although the information you need may not always be available electronically. In some fields, such as the social sciences, information you must read to be informed about your topic may still be published only in print form. This is especially true if you are taking a historical approach to your research. As such, it is useful to understand how information is organized in most academic libraries, and how to locate that information effectively and efficiently.

SEARCHING IN THE INFORMATION AGE

How people access information has changed dramatically since this book was first published in 2000, and even more change has occurred in the past five years. At that time, we presented details on how libraries organize information and how a researcher could retrieve that information easily. Libraries, as physical spaces, are still very important in today's age of information. New and renovated libraries frequently include cafes, computers, and wireless Internet access. In addition, there has been a dramatic shift toward moving information formerly printed in books and paper journals to born digital or reborn digital books and periodicals. The phrase *born digital* means that the information—whether a book or an article—was first created electronically and may or may not be followed up by a print version. *Reborn digital* means that the information was originally produced in print and/or in some other non-print form, such as microfilm or microfiche formats. In these instances, the print and non-print information is converted to electronic form, usually by scanning the information into a computer software program. As a result, where the information is stored and how that information is accessed have changed radically. Therefore, this entire chapter has been revised to present current information-seeking strategies. These strategies will help you hone in and successfully locate the quality information you need.

SEARCHING WISELY

With all the hype about the Internet, people have the misperception that doing a Google search will provide all information needed for a research paper or presentation. At this point in time, this is a myth. Much of what is available on the Internet is done solely as a commercial or entertainment venture. Peer-reviewed journals—journals that connect you with research-based material—are still primarily accessible through subscription-based databases that libraries pay for. There are two trends in accessing scholarly information—open access journals and pay as you go.

Open Access Journals

To counter the increasing subscription costs to access online journals, some entities have begun to publish journals (both peer-reviewed and non-peer-reviewed) as well as conference papers, monographs, book chapters, theses, and other papers for free. Listed through the *Directory of Open Access Journals* (https://doaj.org), individuals and groups worldwide are making this information reusable under the Creative Commons license that provides for free distribution of otherwise copyrighted works.

There is no charge for accessing this information, but cost is still involved. In some instances, the author or sponsor of the research may be required to pay a fee to be published in an open access journal. In other cases, the fee is paid by an academic institution, a government entity, or a learned society. Here, the author does not pay anything. Some open access journals may provide free access, but only after the article has been made available through subscription for six to twelve months. This is known as "embargoing."

Pay As You Go

Another option to access journal articles that publishers are offering is the "pay as you go" model. Under this model, you locate an article that you want to read, and when you click on the article, you may see a message asking you to pay $X to access the article. Cost per article can vary anywhere between $15 to as much as $65 or more. If you do not have the funds to purchase the article directly, check with the library at your college or university. The library may have the article in paper format that you can copy or scan, or you may be able to request the article through interlibrary loan at no or minimal cost.

SCOPE OF THE SOURCE

Good researchers conduct literature searches using a combination of online searching through a library's portal, Internet searches, and tradition library research (e.g., locating and reading materials available only in print format). Before you begin your search, determine the scope of the source that you are searching. In other words, what kind of information will you retrieve from your search? Here are some questions to guide you in selecting sources in either electronic or print form:

- What am I searching?
  - A website?
  - A library online catalog?
  - A database?
  - Multiple databases?
- What kind of information is included?
  - Books?
  - Media (e.g., streaming video, podcasts)?
  - Journals?
  - Magazines?
  - Newspapers?
- What time period does the source cover?
  - How many years does it include?
- How current is the information being searched?
  - How often is it updated?
  - When was it last updated?
  - What information is updated?
- Is the information full text (entire documents)?
  - Or citations and abstracts?
  - Or citations only?
  - Or text with images (e.g., pictures, graphs)?

LIBRARY WEB PORTAL

Almost all academic libraries now have a web portal that provides you access to:

- The library's online catalog
- Databases that the library subscribes to or provides access to
- Digital collections (typically includes items digitized from the library's special collections, such as manuscripts and rare books)

Academic library portals are not all searchable in the same way, nor do they retrieve the same information. Sometimes you will need to search the online library catalog separately from online databases. Other times you will enter your search terms in one search box, and the results you retrieve will include books, e-books, e-journals, print journals, and more. The good thing is that, when you retrieve information on a topic, the type and format of the information will be listed, so that you can easily select an e-book, several e-journals, or other sources without needing to scroll through hundreds of search results.

If the information is available through the library's portal, you should be able to access it. For example, if you find an e-book or e-journal that you want to access, typically you will be prompted to enter your university ID and password. This is because those affiliated with the institution (students, faculty, staff, etc.) can access information paid for by the university, thereby adhering to publisher's licensing agreements. If you find an actual print book that is available in the library's collection, you just need to go to the shelf, find the book, use it in the library, or check it out.

ONLINE LIBRARY CATALOG

Due to advances in technology, a library's online catalog is now one of several options for an online information search. One library's online catalog is as different as the next. Some will give you access only to information found within the library building, such as print books, print journals, media (microforms), and other holdings. Today, more often than not, a library's online catalog provides you access to material found within the library itself, but also gives you links to information found elsewhere online. For example, you may locate a book that is available both in print and electronic format. Depending on your preferences, you can click on the link and obtain immediate access to the e-book or go to the library and check out the actual print book.

In addition, some library catalogs will also provide you access to research guides. Sometimes research guides are referred to as LibGuides. Librarians develop and update LibGuides for almost all subjects offered at your college or university. Accessible through the online library catalog and/or as a separate link from the library portal, these guides provide you with quality information on various topics, such as microbiology, anthropology, nineteenth-century authors, and more. Starting with a research guide will save you time by offering access to the best information available to begin researching your selected topic.

LIBRARY WEBSITE

Academic libraries also maintain their own websites. Here you will not only find access to information in a variety of formats (as described above), you will also find information about the library (e.g., the library's hours, directions to the library, map of the library), current news about the library (e.g., upcoming events, new databases, new exhibits), and links to related sources of information on campus, such as upcoming lectures. In many cases, you can now ask a librarian for assistance online.

Usually, clicking on an icon that says something like "Ask a Librarian" or "Chat with a Librarian" enables you to have an online conversation with a librarian about what type of information you are looking for and the best places to locate that information. Whether you are located within the library or outside the library's walls, you can access a library's web portal, online library catalog, and website as long as you have an electronic device (e.g., smart phone, laptop) with Internet access.

BENTO BOXES

Not to complicate searching for information too much, but a word needs to be said about bento boxes. In the Japanese language, the word *bento* actually translates to "lunch box." It is not clear how this word came to be connected with online searching for information; however, it is important to know that a bento box is essentially one search box in which you enter key words. In academic library lingo, the bento box is federated searching. Federated searching is when the search box (the bento box) pulls information from various sources, such as journal articles, book, e-books, or websites. Algorithms are used to retrieve this information. Unfortunately, it is not clear at this time which algorithms are used. A good example is searching Google. When you retrieve information from a Google search, you do not know if the items retrieved are listed by cost, peer review, customer searching preferences, or something else. (You are probably familiar with customer searching. This is when you search for an item online and the algorithm keeps track of the items you are interested in, then automatically feeds you additional options that you see when viewing your social media or when visiting various websites.) Customer searching models are providing you with the information that the search thinks you need, but may not be exactly what you are looking for.

According to Jackson (2017), there are search engines besides Google that do not track your searches. A few of these are StartPage, Oscobo, and GoodGopher. Semantic Scholar (https://www.semanticscholar.org/) is a free search engine that retrieves information from research papers, and articles, as well as finding authors, figures, and references within journals and other sources. Semantic Scholar provides you with peer-reviewed research information. It also shows, in timeline graph form, the frequency of published information on your topic over years and decades. It is anticipated that more academic libraries will implement bento box searching as it improves over time.

INFORMATION ORGANIZED:
LIBRARY OF CONGRESS CLASSIFICATION

There is no question that it is easiest to go online and search for information. Another excellent place to start your search, however, is going to the library and browsing through the book collection. An initial browsing of your library's bookshelves may reveal much relevant information for your research project.

Materials in libraries have been selected by librarians and professors who are experts or have strong interests in specific topics. In other words, books in a library's collection are selected to meet your learning needs. Chances are you will locate a book or two that contains a chapter on your research topic just by browsing the collection. Browsing a collection can go rather quickly if you are familiar with how books are organized. Almost all college and university libraries shelve their book collections according to the Library of Congress Classification (LCC) system. In contrast, most school and public libraries use the Dewey Decimal Classification (DDC) system. The aim of both is the same: to arrange books on shelves according to the topics covered within them. Our focus here is on the LCC system. One can go from college library to college library, find one particular section (such as the BF section), and locate books on psychology. LC Classification organizes books by subject. Similar subjects are shelved together, making browsing an attractive option.

Table 3.1 shows the general outline of the LCC scheme. It is a good idea to be familiar with the LCC scheme as, frequently, sociological topics are cross-disciplinary. This means that books and materials on your topic may not only be found in the H section of the library (sociology), but in other sections as well. For example, if your topic is "Do men who abuse women have a much stronger genetic predisposition toward alcoholism than do men who do not physically abuse women?" you may explore materials found in the H section (see Table 3.2) but also in the R section (medicine) and the B section (psychology).

Table 3.1   Library of Congress Classification Outline

A	General Works
B–BJ	Philosophy, Psychology
BL–BX	Religion
C–D	History
E–F	American History
G	Geography, Anthropology, and Sports
H–HJ	Social Sciences: Economics
HM–HX	Social Sciences: Sociology
J	Political Science
K	Law
L	Education
M	Music
N	Fine Arts
P–PZ	Languages and Literature
Q	Science
R	Medicine
S	Agriculture
T	Technology
U	Military Science
V	Naval Science
Z	Bibliography, Library Science

Table 3.2.   Library of Congress Classification Section for the Social Sciences

HM	Sociology
HM 251–291	Social Psychology
HN	Social History, Social Problems, Social Reform
HQ	Family, Marriage, Women
HQ 503–1064	Adultery, The Aged, Child Study, Divorce
HQ 1101–2030	Women, Feminism
HS	Societies (Religious, Ethnic, Political)
HT	Communities, Classes, Races
HT 101–384	Urban Sociology, Cities and Towns
HT 601–1445	Social Classes
HT 1501–1595	Races
HV	Social Pathology, Social and Public Welfare, Criminology
HV 5001–5729	Alcoholism
HV 5725–5770	Tobacco Habit
HV 5800–5840	Drug Habits, Drug Abuse
HV 6001–9920	Criminology
HV 6251–7220	Crimes and Offenses
HV 7231–9920	Police, Prisons, Punishment, Reform, Juvenile Delinquency
HX	Socialism, Communism, Anarchism

FINDING THE BOOK ON THE SHELF

The letter(s) along with numbers will appear on the spine (side) of the book as a call number. Each book in the library has a unique call number. You can think of a call number as the "address" for a book. Call numbers can be written in two ways:

HV 554 .G3 2018   This form is found in most online library catalogs.

HV   This form is found as a call number on the spine (side) of
554   the book.
.G3
2018

Locating a book on the shelf is easy if you take the process one step at a time. Start with the first letter or letters in the call number:

H   HC   HF   HV

Next, look at the second line of numbers:

HV   HV   HV   HV
5   50   554   570

Then, look at the third line of a letter and number(s):

HV	HV	HV	HV
5	50	554	570
.A4	.K12	.G3	.Z20

Finally, look at the last line, which gives the year of publication:

HV	HV	HV	HV
5	50	554	570
.A4	.K12	.G3	.Z20
1997	1993	2018	1980

REFERENCE BOOKS: PRINT AND ELECTRONIC

Basically, reference books (online or in print) contain materials that you can "refer" to as needed. Materials in this category can be encyclopedias (e.g., Wikipedia), dictionaries, handbooks, statistical sources, laws, speeches, and so on. Reference books are a great way to read a summary of major landmark studies that have been published on your topic, and to obtain statistics to help you understand your research question. You can access reference titles via a Google search, via a library's online portal, or by going to the library itself. Most library buildings have a separate section where they shelve reference books. No matter what format the reference material is in, you need to read this information with a critical eye for accuracy and reliability. More information about how to evaluate the information you find for quality can be found at the end of Chapter 4. Following are some of the more useful reference titles in the social sciences. This is not a comprehensive list. New books are made available electronically and in print often. This list will get you started locating background information on your topic. If you need assistance with locating reference titles, in print or online, ask a librarian.

Baumeister, Roy F., & Vohs, Kathleen D. (Eds). (2007). *Encyclopedia of social psychology.* Los Angeles, CA: Sage.

Borgatta, E. F., & Montgomery, R. J. (Eds). (2000). *Encyclopedia of sociology.* New York, NY: MacMillan. (Available online through a subscription.)

Diagnostic and statistical manual of mental disorders: DSM-5. (2013). Washington, DC: American Psychiatric Association (available online through a subscription.)

Kuper, A., & Kuper, J. (Eds). (2009). *The social science encyclopedia.* New York, NY: Routledge.

PDR prescribers' digital reference. (2017). Whippany, NJ: ConnectiveRx. https://www.pdr.net/ (PDR Search replaces *Physician's Desk Reference*, which is no longer published in book format. PDR Search is free).

Piotrowski, N. A. (Ed). (2003). *International encyclopedia of social science: Psychology.* Hackensack, NJ: Salem Press.

Ponzetti, J. (Ed). (2003). *International encyclopedia of marriage and the family.* New York, NY: Macmillan Reference USA.

Publication manual of the American Psychological Association, 6th edition. (2009). Washington, DC: APA.

Ritzer, George, & Ryan, J. Michael. (Eds). (2011). *The concise encyclopedia of sociology.* New York, NY: Wiley-Blackwell.

Schulz, Richard. (Ed). (2006). *Encyclopedia of aging,* 4th edition. New York, NY: Springer.

Stearns, P. N. (Ed). (2006). *Encyclopedia of social history.* New York, NY: Taylor & Francis.

ONLINE SEARCH COMMANDS

Most of us have searched Google or another online source, and either retrieved links to thousands of pieces of information (some of it relevant, most of it not) or found no information relevant to our research needs. You can use online search commands to your advantage to either expand or narrow and further refine your search.

Almost all sites on the Internet that provide a search box to enter in key words will have search commands that you can use. The most common types of commands are known as Boolean search operators.

Boolean Search Operators

A Boolean search operator is a word that connects key words in a way that the database or online resource recognizes. The most common Boolean search operators are AND, OR, and NOT. You can use these words in various combinations to refine your search. Using the research question "Is violence in dating relationships conceptually distinct from violence in marital relationships?" search examples include:

dating OR marriage — retrieves information about dating or marriage. This is a very broad search.

dating AND marriage — retrieves information about dating and about marriage. Both the words *dating* and *marriage* need to appear in your search. This is a much more refined search than using the Boolean operator OR.

dating NOT marriage — retrieves information about dating but not about marriage. The NOT operator excludes the words that follow it.

Note that some websites and databases apply default Boolean operators to a search string. For example, typing in *dating marriage* may return results for either dating OR marriage or dating AND marriage. It is a good idea to read the website or database help screens to determine if the system you are searching uses default Boolean operators.

Case Sensitivity

Unlike typing in your ID and password to gain access to a system, most Internet and database searches are not case sensitive. This means that you can type in your search in all lowercase letters or in all UPPERCASE LETTERS. You can even type your search eItHeR WaY.

Limiting

Almost all online searches or other electronic resources allow you to limit your search in various ways. These include limiting your search by year or years, language, document type (journal, report, etc.), author, journal title, date, and so on. Check the help screens to see which limiting capabilities are available.

Truncation

Truncation means that you can type in the root of a word and place a truncation symbol at the end of the word to retrieve variations of that word. For example, typing in *relat** will retrieve *relation, relationships, related,* and any other words beginning with *relat*. Symbols used for truncation are not standard across different databases. More common symbols that you will see used for truncation are:

- relat* (asterisk)
- relat? (question mark)
- relat# (pound sign)
- relat: (colon)

READING HELP SCREENS

In reality, no one likes to take time to read the help screens when searching online for information. However, good help screens can provide you with tips for conducting an effective search, especially when your search is not providing the information you need. Help screens should give you several important pieces of information, including whether the database is case sensitive or insensitive, the truncation symbol to use, Boolean operators to use, and sample searches on which you can model your own search. A quick scan of help pages when you are stuck with your search can save you time and enable you to retrieve more relevant information.

SEARCHING DATABASES FOR
SCHOLARLY JOURNAL ARTICLES

There are many online resources that you can search to obtain access to scholarly journal articles on your research topic. Because there are so many choices, you may want to ask your professor or librarian to suggest the best database(s) to search. Another option is to go to your library's website and see if a librarian has categorized the available databases by subject. For example, using the research topic of abused women, if you were interested in exploring this subject from a sociological point of view, you may elect to search the Social Sciences Full Text database. If you were interested in exploring this subject from a historical point of view, you might want to search JSTOR (a database of back issues of scholarly journals in history, political science, demography, etc. Read more about JSTOR later in this chapter.) Remember that one library may subscribe to databases that another library may not. Frequently, the online resources available through your college or university library are selected by librarians and professors in key subject areas studied by you, the student, as well as by researchers connected to the campus. You should be confident that you will find at least one database to search through your library's website. If you cannot find one, ask a librarian for assistance.

Searching an online database for journal articles is much the same as doing a Google search. You select a database to search through your library's website by clicking on the name of the database itself. At this point, you may be asked to input an ID number and password. Why? Libraries subscribe to databases that contain scholarly journal articles—meaning that the library at your campus paid money to a database company so that you, the student, and faculty can access this information. Librarians need a way to control who has access to databases in order to meet the requirements of licensing agreements they sign with database companies. An easy way of doing this is to have each person input his or her own unique ID number and password. By inputting an ID and password, you will be authenticated, or allowed to access the database. If you do not have an ID and password, ask a librarian or your computer center for help.

Once you have been allowed access to the database, you will have options for doing a basic search or an advanced search. Most basic searches are those where you input your key words. For example, if you are searching for information on the question "Is violence in dating relationships conceptually distinct from violence in marital relationships?" you might enter this basic search: *violence* AND (*dating* OR *marriage*). If this basic search yields too much information, you can narrow your query by conducting an advanced search. Advanced searching allows you to limit your search by year; use Boolean operators such as AND, OR, and NOT; or restrict your search results to the full text of a journal article, an abstract and citations for the article, or the citations alone. Here is what an advanced search may look like, using the previous example: *violence* AND (*dating* OR *marriage*). You could limit further by a range of years (e.g., 2010–2018) and by type of information (e.g., full-text journal articles). Again, these options vary from database to database, but most databases generally provide you with these choices.

There are questions to ask yourself when you are searching a database for journal articles:

- Which journal titles are included in the database? This varies from database to database depending upon the subject(s) covered as well as licensing agreements between each journal publisher and the company that creates the database itself.

Some databases may cover only those journals in a specific subject area, such as psychology. Other databases may be broader in scope, covering several subject areas. You may also find the same journal title accessible via several databases. (Think of what is offered via Netflix vs. HBO vs. Showtime.) The best approach is to click on the journal title list that is available in the database. The journal title list is usually on the same page where you input your key words to conduct a basic search. You can quickly skim the journal title list to see if the database contains the types of journals you are interested in reading.

- What is the coverage, in terms of years, of the database? For example, does the database cover the most recent five years of journals? Or does the database go back ten or fifteen years? More? Sometimes you will have the option of searching a database that contains the most recent articles, as well as searching a second database of the same name but containing older articles. A database that contains such articles is sometimes referred to as "back files" or as a retrospective database.
- What is the "lag time" of the database? Most databases have a lag time between the date that the journal article is published to the date that the journal article actually appears in the database. The lag time could be a week, a month, every quarter, or yearly. This is important if you are searching for a very recent article. For example, you may be searching for an article that appears in the August 2018 issue of *Social Casework*. The database you are searching may only include journal articles up to June 30, 2018. If this happens, ask a librarian if the library subscribes to an e-version or print version of the journal. If it does, you can locate it online or find it on the shelf in the library.
- Is the database full text? Partially full text? Abstract and citation? Or citation only? Most people assume that all databases contain the complete text of each article. This is a misunderstanding. Some databases are full text—meaning that the full text of each journal is included in the database. If this is the case, you only need to search the online resource for articles on your topic, find your articles, and either print them out or email/download them to your computer or to an account you may have in the cloud. Some databases are partially full text. This means that you might find the full text of an article you seek, or you will retrieve the complete citation to the article along with an abstract, or just the citation to the article. An abstract is usually a 250-word or shorter paragraph summarizing the key points of the journal article. If you retrieve a citation to an article along with an abstract or just a citation, you can search the library's online portal to see if the library has the article in another form (e.g., in print) or if you can obtain the article through interlibrary loan. Sometimes databases contain only citations to articles found in journals. This means that you will retrieve the information needed to locate the article: the author(s) of the article, article title, journal title, issue date, volume and issue numbers, and page numbers. See later sections for more information on how to obtain articles when you only have a citation and abstract or just a citation to go by.

Comparing Databases

Knowing what information is included (as well as excluded) in various online resources will greatly assist you in your search for information. Below is a brief example of the kind of information you will find when comparing databases. These databases are those available through the American Psychological Association (APA).

- PsycBOOKS is a database containing thousands of titles of peer-reviewed books that also includes reference titles published by the APA. It is updated monthly, with texts going back to the 1600s.
- PsycEXTRA includes access to sometimes difficult-to-locate information found in conference proceedings, reports, newsletters, brochures, fact sheets, and more. It is updated biweekly with new developments in psychological and behavioral sciences research.
- PsycINFO provides access to peer-reviewed research and is considered the most comprehensive resource for the field of psychology. It includes more than fifty years of journal articles, book chapters and reviews, clinical case reports, empirical studies, and literature reviews.

A word of caution here: most researchers (students and faculty alike) prefer to take the path of least resistance when searching for information. People are more apt to select journal articles or books that are immediately available to them: the first entry on a Google search, or the full-text journal article in a database. However, you may want to retrieve an article that is directly on point for your topic, but the database only gives you a citation to the article rather than the complete text of the article. The same is true for a book. You may have a citation to a book, but you may only be able to access a portion of that book online and your library may not have the book on the shelf. Instead of changing your topic to come in line with the books or journal articles that are readily available, obtain the article through your library's interlibrary loan service. (More information on interlibrary loan is at the end of this chapter.) If you do this, you will end up with a more satisfying research paper or project rather than writing a paper on a topic that you are not really interested in.

A Word About JSTOR

JSTOR initially started as a solution to the shortage of shelf space that many libraries experience. Most academic libraries have back issues of a number of journal titles, some going back a few years, with many going back one hundred years and more! Created by William G. Bowe, president of the Andrew W. Mellon Foundation, the concept of JSTOR sought to alleviate the shortage of shelf space in libraries while giving libraries another option for preserving their journals and enhancing access to articles found within these journals. As such, those libraries that participate in JSTOR have their journals scanned electronically into a searchable database.

Access to JSTOR is available only if you are a student, faculty, or researcher associated with an institution that participates in JSTOR, via a subscription that your library may have, or through an individual subscription account. Institutions located in the United States as well as countries around the world participate in JSTOR, providing access to many scholarly journals, such as the *American Journal of Sociology* and the *American Sociological Review*. JSTOR is best used when searching older journals, with several dating back to the 1800s!

Additional Search Suggestions

Depending on your research topic, you may search more than one database. Searching for information can be considered a controlled trial-and-error process. You begin by identifying possible key words to locate information on your topic. Using these key words and their synonyms, you select databases that include journals on your subject area to search. Be open to using different combinations of your key words and synonyms, limiting your search by year(s), and truncating roots of words. Remember, there is no perfect search! Librarians and researchers find information using the methods explained in this text. Sometimes the first search works; sometimes it doesn't. Keep trying key words, synonyms, and the last names of experts in the subject field you are researching. In this manner, your search for information is not a wild goose chase, nor is it so confined as to be inflexible. You have established intellectual boundaries within which you can use combinations of words to locate the information you seek.

OBTAINING INFORMATION
THROUGH INTERLIBRARY LOAN

Taking advantage of a library's interlibrary loan service opens up an entire world of information to you. Interlibrary loan is just that—the loaning of materials between libraries for the people who use libraries. Most interlibrary loan services are free. However, some libraries may charge a modest fee. You can use interlibrary loan to obtain books or journal articles that are not available in your library. Books can usually be borrowed for several weeks. Journal articles, as well as chapter(s) in books, are usually scanned and sent to you electronically. Journal articles and book chapters do not need to be returned, but you do need to return the books. Note that other media (e.g., videos, CDs, DVDs) may or may not be available through your library's interlibrary loan service.

Below is a generic example of searching one database for journal articles on dating and marital violence. For the purposes of this example, consider the database to be one that contains citations to journal articles in the social sciences. Entering the following search into a database will retrieve information with the words *women* or *woman* and *dating* or *marriage* or *marital* and *violence* or *violent*.

SUBJECT WORDS: women or woman

SECOND SUBJECT: dat: or mar:

THIRD SUBJECT: violen:

PERSON'S NAME:

TITLE WORDS:

JOURNAL NAME:

YEAR:

This search originally yielded twenty-seven citations to scholarly journal articles and book reviews on the topic. The following is one citation from this search.

AUTHOR: Carlson, Bonnie E.

TITLE: Dating violence: A research review and comparison with spouse abuse

SOURCE: Social Casework (ISSN: 0037-7678) v 68 p 16–23 (January 1987)

SUBJECTS COVERED: Women/United States/Crimes against; Dating violence; Wife abuse

Reading this citation is easy and straightforward. The author is Bonnie E. Carlson. The title of the journal article is "Dating Violence: A Research Review and Comparison with Spouse Abuse." This article appears in the journal *Social Casework*, volume 68, in the January 1987 issue, on pages 16–23. Subjects covered in this article include crimes against women in the United States, dating violence, and wife abuse. The ISSN is the International Standard Serial Number that is used by libraries to locate this journal electronically through interlibrary loan. This citation seems very pertinent to the research question, as the article discusses both dating violence and marital violence, so it would be a good article to locate and read.

To see if your library subscribes to or provides access to this issue of *Social Casework*, the database you are searching may automatically provide a link to this particular issue. In that case, just click on the link. The database you are searching may indicate that your library does not provide access to this journal title. If you do not see any such indication, search the title of the journal (Social Casework) in the library's portal or online library catalog.

Remember to check specifically for the volume you need (volume 68), the January 1987 issue, and pages 16–23. The library online catalog or library portal will tell you whether the journal title is available online and/or in print, or just in print in the library; or it will indicate that the library does not have this journal title (or it may have the journal title, but not the exact issue you need). If the journal title is available online, just click on the link; if it is only available in print, locate it in the library and scan it or make a paper copy (usually for a nominal fee per page); or if the library does not have the journal title or issue you need, then you can electronically request the article through interlibrary loan.

Requesting an article, book, or other material through interlibrary loan is easy. Most times you will complete a form online through the library's web portal or online library catalog. You will be asked to input what is known as the bibliographic information for the item you are requesting. For a book, this will be the author(s), book title, and place of publication, publisher, and date of publication. The interlibrary loan form may also ask for the ISBN of the book. (This is the International Standard Book Number; similar to the ISSN for a journal, the ISBN allows librarians to search for the book title by this number.) You may also need to input where you found the bibliographic information. For example, if you retrieved the citation for the book from a database, you would indicate, "Located in [title of database]." For a journal article, you would input the author(s), the title of the article, the title of the journal, the volume number and issue number (if available), the date of the issue, and the page numbers of the article. You may also be asked to add the ISSN of the journal title.

Once that information is completed, you will add your name, email address, phone number, and possibly your university or college ID number, then press the submit button. Within a day or so you should receive the status of your interlibrary loan request. Most online library systems will allow you to check the status of your request (similar to online tracking of packages) so that you will be able to see when the article is expected to be emailed to you or instructions for you to access it online, or when the actual book is available for you to pick up. Some libraries will send the book to a location on campus for you to retrieve, and some will mail the book to your address.

Go to Appendix C and complete Worksheet 6: Locating Books, and Worksheet 8: Locating Scholarly Articles.

4

Evaluating the Information You Find

Due to the dramatic increase of "fake news" and false information over the past several years, it is important to include an entire chapter that addresses the best strategies for evaluating information. Today, there is not only an issue of information overload coming at us in all kinds of formats (e.g., text, video, audio, or in real time), this issue is compounded by the researcher needing to sift through information to determine what information is credible and what information is inaccurate. Learning about filter bubbles and using the CRAAP (yes, that is what it is called) test will enable you to determine usable information.

FILTER BUBBLES

Filter bubbles are created by algorithms designed to serve up information that sites on the Internet believe you want. In very basic terms, an algorithm is a sequence of specific actions designed to solve an issue. Some search engines have algorithms designed to use search strings (or key words, Boolean operators, and limiters [e.g., year, format, type] you input into a search engine) to search for information accessible online. Marketing, social media, and Internet search engine experts create algorithms in an attempt to anticipate what information you want. The argument to use algorithms is to try and personalize the information you retrieve so that you locate relevant information quickly. (It is also designed to help companies target market to individuals interested in purchasing various products and services.)

The algorithms are described as serving up information within a "bubble" by analyzing your search history, where you have browsed on the Internet, and which websites you have visited. You may have already seen filter bubbles in action by seeing advertisements for items you just looked for and social media sites you have recently interacted with or read.

In this attempt to provide you with specific information, a filter bubble actually isolates your search by giving you information it thinks you need rather than the information you may actually want. Essentially, a filter bubble is trying to do the critical thinking for you. When searching for information online, it is important to be aware of the potential influence filter bubbles may have on your research. This requires vigilance. Reviewing your personalized search and privacy settings on the browsers and social media websites you use, as well as using search engines that do not employ algorithms (as described in the previous chapter), will enable *you* to determine whether or not the information you retrieve is actually the information that you need.

THE CRAAP TEST

Yes, there is a test you can apply to help determine the relevance of the information that you retrieve and, yes, it is called the CRAAP test. The CRAAP test helps you decide if the information is current, relevant, authoritative, accurate, and serves the original purpose for developing the information.

Here are the primary elements to use when applying the CRAAP test to any information that you are evaluating:

- *Currency*: This is to determine when the information was created. Ask yourself: What is the copyright, publication, and/or posting date? Is the information outdated for the research you are doing? Does the date matter to your research?
- *Relevance*: This is to determine whether the information is applicable to your research. Ask yourself: For what audience was this information written (e.g., the general public, experts, scholars)? At what level is the information presented (e.g., elementary level, intermediate level, more advanced level)? Consider whether you would use and/or quote the information in your research.
- *Authority*: This is to determine if the information you retrieve has been created by a reliable source. To decide on authority, ask yourself: Who are the authors or sources of the information? Are they experts? Are they credible? Does the author(s) provide evidence of professional affiliation(s) (such as being on faculty at a university, or a member of a professional association)? Review the credibility of the institution or organization. Is it a real, bona fide institution? Remember that any person and any organization on the Internet can claim expertise. If you have any questions about the authority of a source, do some more research to find out if the author or source is, in fact, an authority on the topic(s).
- *Accuracy*: With the prevalence of "fake news" today, it is important for you to determine whether the information you find is correct, truthful, and can be

considered reliable. Ask yourself: What kind of language is being used? Is the tone of the text, images, or other material subjective, emotional, or professional?

• *Purpose*: This is to discover what the main purpose of the information is. Ask yourself: Why does this information exist? Is it to share research and new knowledge? Is it to educate, to persuade, or to entertain? Consider the affiliation of the author(s) and the organization(s). Do their connections slant the information and point of view presented?

You can use the CRAAP test any time you are reading or viewing information, regardless of format. It does not matter if the information is online, in print, visual, audio, or all of the above—the CRAAP test applies to all types of information in all formats. So use this test to your advantage.

ASKING FOR ASSISTANCE

As stated earlier in this book, you may feel a bit overwhelmed by the sources available to you in your information search. There is the Internet, databases, streaming video, social media, news feeds, and so on. Some information can be accessed freely, and some require payment.

It is ok to ask for assistance at any time during the research process—from the beginning when you are formulating a research question, through the search and evaluation process, right through to the end when you are working on a research paper or presentation. Do not hesitate to ask a librarian for help. Librarians at academic institutions hold master's (graduate) degrees in the field of library and information science. In graduate school, librarians learn how to search for information and where to locate the best information on a topic. A librarian can be your link between a topic and the information you need. At most libraries, you can contact a librarian in several ways: by walking into the library and asking for assistance, by phoning the library, and via the Internet through the library's web portal using email and chat services. Some libraries are staffed with librarians who may have a second master's degree in a specific field of study, such as criminal justice or political science, and some may also hold doctoral (PhD), law (JD), or medical (MD) degrees. These librarians are considered subject specialists—meaning that they have more in-depth knowledge on specific topics. You can usually make an appointment (online, via phone, or in person). This individual research consultation can be very useful to you, especially if you have a detailed project to research. If you make an appointment for a consultation, make sure that you come prepared with specific questions you need answers to, as well as some sense of the type of information you are seeking (e.g., online resources, journal articles, videos, or books).

Note that not all library reference services are available 24/7. If the chat service is not available, send an email. Most librarians will respond to your question within twenty-four hours (longer on the weekends and holidays). You should be able to locate a list of subjects for which specific librarians are experts on the library's web portal. If you are searching for subject-specific information, such as topics in social work or history, look for the librarian for that subject. Contact information should be available so that you may contact that librarian directly.

Take time to complete Worksheet 9: Evaluating Information in Appendix C.

5

Outlining the Research Paper

Before you can really begin outlining your paper, you should have a sense of what information is available. As you look through the literature, you will begin identifying some issues. Because your paper cannot possibly be exhaustive—you cannot cover everything—you may have to refocus your research question. You will need to identify areas of information that address your question, and limit your paper to a few of these. We call these *key points*. For instance, in the example paper in Appendix B, the research question posed is: "Is violence in dating relationships conceptually distinct from violence in marital relationships?" This question is asked from a sociological perspective, and will be examining dating violence as a form of intimate violence. There is so much information on dating violence that the focus must necessarily be limited. Bring yourself wholeheartedly into the decision-making process regarding the direction of your own research, and decide which areas or key points you will address. Do not expect to cover everything, or you will soon become overwhelmed.

Choose key points that make sense together. You definitely want to review a lot of information about a few points rather than a little information about many points. When you try to cover too many areas, your research paper or presentation starts to look more like a checklist rather than a well-thought-out research review. Remember: Your professors can tell the difference! Also remember: Your professors have been where you are now!

You will soon find in your literature review that, in order to have a comprehensive response to your question, you need to review and include literature that does not focus on, or possibly does not even address, your specific topic. By the same token, you will find that much of the literature written on your primary topic of interest is not relevant for your own research. If for no other reason than this, plan on reviewing a lot of literature and going into areas related to, but not necessarily focused on, your topic. You will be able to make some interesting connections between various pieces of information that relate directly to your question, and will add substance to your paper. Once again, you will be using your own critical-thinking skills to bring the various pieces together in a way that makes sense. This is a creative and challenging process. In time, and with practice, you will find the process enjoyable and enlightening. At the very least, it will certainly come to seem less onerous and intimidating.

It should be clear by now that before you can produce an effective outline, you must have a working knowledge of the literature. Once you have this working knowledge and before you go extensively into the next step, which is called "taking notes while reading," you are ready to form an outline. A rough or preliminary outline is essential because it will help you not only organize and write your paper, but also guide your search for relevant information. To give you an idea of what goes into developing an outline, an example of the process involved in outlining the example paper in Appendix B is provided here. You may also follow this procedure to prepare a presentation or poster session. (Please refer to Chapter 9 for more details on preparing a presentation and a poster.)

THE OUTLINE

Introduction

Always have an introduction to your paper. The introduction must include your specific research question. You should also state the specific key points that you will be covering, in the order that you will address these. You might include some fundamental information in the introduction, such as why this is an important area to study—a brief explanation will do—and how many people are affected by your topic. If not specified in the introduction, you should include somewhere in your paper or presentation how many people are impacted by your topic—basic statistical information—and do not forget to cite where that information comes from. If different sources provide different statistics, that is perfectly acceptable; simply state the differences. At some point you may want to include an explanation of why different resources provide different figures. This can possibly be an integral part of your paper. (For a final paper example of an introduction, see Appendix B, paragraph 1.)

Key Point 1

Begin listing the main parts of key point 1. In the final paper, you will have a review of the literature focused on this first point (see Appendix B, paragraphs 2 through 4).

Key Point 2

Begin listing the main parts of key point 2. In the final paper, you will have a review of the literature focused on this second point (see Appendix B, paragraphs 5 through 7).

Key Point 3

Begin listing the main parts of key point 3. In the final paper, you will have a review of the literature focused on this third point (see Appendix B, paragraphs 11 through 12).

Conclusion

Always have a conclusion. At the very least, this should sum up the paper. You may provide some of your own insights—always based on the literature review. You may make suggestions for further research in this area (see Appendix B, paragraph 12).

REFERENCES

The American Psychological Association (APA) refers to the full citations of all sources cited in the text as a reference list. Every source cited in the text must have its full citation in the reference list, and every full citation in the reference list must be cited at least once in the text of your paper. If you are using the APA format for citing resources (explained in Chapter 7), then you should not include any uncited sources in the reference list pages.

You may keep a working bibliography, which is a more comprehensive reading list but not the same as a reference list. The outline becomes a working guideline for you. Some sections become longer and more complex than other sections, which is fine. Your paper should have the necessary information to introduce the reader to the problems under consideration. In our case, key point 1 and key point 2 provide a foundation for examining the research question in more depth. Undergoing the process of outlining the paper helps you to organize the literature you have been reviewing. The outline might be considered a work in progress, as you will probably revise it as you go along. Note the list of authors and the years in which their works were written. These are the authors whose research will be included in the paper. The same author may be included in different parts of the paper as the source material applies. You may have more authors (or different authors) listed in the outline than you will actually cite in the final research paper.

Unless there is a compelling reason to do otherwise, you should present studies and events in chronological order. Thus, it would be more sensible to present early, "classical" research on your topic first, followed by more contemporary, recent research. If, however, for reasons of individual style or effect you wish to refer to the most recent study and then work your way backward, there is no firm rule against doing so.

EXAMPLE PROCESS OF DEVELOPING AN OUTLINE

In developing key points to be focused on in your paper, you will probably find that your topic needs to be understood within a larger context. This might be a good place to start. How does your topic fit into a larger field of study? In researching dating violence, it soon becomes clear that this is one area of study within the larger field of family violence.

The Outline

Introduction

Research Question: Is violence in dating relationships conceptually distinct from violence in marital relationships?

Key point 1: Dating violence may be understood as a form of family violence or, more precisely, intimate violence.

Key point 2: The role of dating and courtship in society must be examined.

Key point 3: Dating violence may be understood as being conceptually distinct from violence between spouses and cohabiting partners.

Key point 1: Dating violence may be understood as a form of family violence or, more precisely, intimate violence.

   A. Dating violence research is one area of study within a larger field of family violence.

     1. Short history of research on family violence

     2. Extent of family violence (Straus & Gelles, 1990; Steinmetz, 1977–1978)

       a. Family violence research laboratory

       b. Violence by men toward women

       c. Violence by parents toward children

       d. Violence by women toward men

     3. Theoretical focus of research not limited to male domination and female subordination (Stets & Pirog-Good, 1989; Lobel, 1986)

   B. Violence between intimate others is not limited to married couples.

Key point 2: The role of dating and courtship in society must be examined.

   A. Research on dating violence demonstrates the need to recognize violence that occurs in dating and courtship (Makepeace, 1981)

   B. There is a romantic love complex (Clausen, 1986; Lott, 1987)

Key point 3: Dating violence is understood as being conceptually distinct from violence between spouses and cohabiting partners.

   A. Research links childhood violence, dating violence, and marital violence (Makepeace, 1981, 1989; Roscoe & Benaske, 1985; Stets & Straus, 1990)

   B. Define the terms dating, cohabiting, and marriage as used in the research on violence (Burke, Stets, & Pirog-Good, 1988; Carlson, 1987; Dobash & Dobash, 1979; Makepeace, 1981; Martin, 1976; Stets & Straus, 1990; Sugarman & Hotaling, 1989)

    C. Explore the structure of the relationship and the extent or type of violence used (Stets & Straus, 1990)

Conclusion

Reference List

In essence, then, our three key points tie together well and seem to adequately address our research question. The paper focuses on some very basic information in the field of dating violence. It provides a foundation for us to build our understanding of the social context of dating violence. This focus also provides us with a fundamental understanding of history of the research on dating violence as it developed within the overall field of family violence. Please note that it can be extremely beneficial for you to review the history of research on your particular area of interest, to build your expertise in the subject area.

    After reading this chapter, locate Worksheet 10: Outlining the Research Paper in Appendix C, and begin filling it in.

6

Taking Notes While Reading

You will be examining a number of sources for your paper. These sources may be primary sources, secondary sources, or tertiary sources. Primary sources are articles, books, or other types of original work, such as diaries and manuscripts, which are written by the original researcher on original work. These primary resources are, of course, preferable to secondary or tertiary sources. However, sometimes you cannot locate the primary sources on a particular study or data set. If you have made an earnest attempt to locate the original source but have been unable to do so, it is acceptable to use a secondary source that alludes to the original research. You must, however, make it clear that you have referenced from a secondary rather than a primary source. Secondary sources refer to the work of others, such as is found in books that provide an overview of literature on a particular topic or in the literature review section of an article. Tertiary sources refer to a source's source—three times removed from the original source. Reference resources, such as encyclopedias, are considered tertiary sources. For your own research, you may use a tertiary resource for guidance. You should not, however, rely on that source for your own research. Rely most heavily on primary and secondary sources. You will eventually find that you want a heavy emphasis on primary sources.

WHAT YOU SHOULD LOOK
FOR IN JOURNAL ARTICLES

You should include information from scientific and/or peer-reviewed journal articles in your research paper. Reading these articles is time consuming and requires a bit of technical skill. Being familiar with the format of the article is very beneficial. Undergraduate students are often mystified by their first exposure to scholarly, professional journal articles. They may contain jargon, references to statistical analysis procedures that seem incomprehensible, and complex, sophisticated theories that the student has not heard of. Keep in mind the following rule: Do not report on something that you do not understand! However, do not put an article aside because you do not want to take the time to comprehend it. Distinguish between articles that are too difficult for you to understand versus those that simply require extra time and effort. Put aside the difficult articles, and continue.

Scholarly journal articles usually begin with an abstract, which is a very short summary of the article itself. Start by reading this summary. If the article appears to be on your topic and of interest to you, read on.

In reading the article, you should try to break it down into sections. Most likely—unless the article is actually a broad survey of past literature or a literature review article—the article is reporting on primary research; that is, research conducted by the author(s). This makes the article a primary source, and that is what we are concerned with now. Note that the article may be written by one or more authors.

Journal articles are usually written in a sequence that follows the methods for carrying out a study. This is generally referred to as the *scientific method*. While this book is not the place to learn all of the possibilities for carrying out a study, we can give you some guidelines for reading the articles that result in such studies. In fact, in order to conduct good research following the steps of the scientific method, the authors must conduct a literature review. To conduct your own literature review using journal articles, you must understand the basics (at least) of the scientific method.

The Scientific Method

The scientific method can be broken down into specific parts. These are the foundation, the research design and data collection, data analysis, and conclusions. If the article has a section called methodology, this probably incorporates both research design and data collection.

The foundation, often called the introduction, really sets the stage for all that is to come in the article. In the foundation, the question is established—what the author wants to study and understand. A review of the literature explains why the problem is an important one to understand, what other people know, and where the gaps are in the research. The author(s) may introduce a theoretical understanding of the problem in this section. The theoretical piece is the key to how the author or authors approach and conceptualize their research question. If there is a hypothesis, it is usually derived from a combination of the research question, the literature review, and the theory. Very simply, a hypothesis is a statement that is going to be tested using empirical data. Empirical data is information that can be gathered using the methods of science, information that can be observed in some fashion. There may not be a hypothesis if the research is exploratory in nature. An exploratory study seeks to find out as much as possible about a topic so that more specific questions may be asked. The study may also be descriptive. In this case, the study tries to describe the problem as much as possible. Because the goal of science is to explain and predict, the study should contribute to this goal in some way. Explanation and prediction ultimately involve theory.

The research design or methodology section describes how the researcher is gathering information for a study. It may involve experimentation, survey research, participant observation, historical data, or other types of data collection. The possibilities are numerous. You should be familiar with the research design in each article. Note whether the author(s) are conducting an experiment or a survey. Is the author a participant observer, or collecting historical or archival data, or something else? Understanding how data is collected is very important in evaluating the study. The author(s) should also generally explain what the limitations are in any given analysis. Limitations do not make a study invalid—indeed, they are inevitable. However, noting the limitations helps guide the reader to an informed understanding of the generalizability of the study.

The data analysis section will cause students the most grief. This section is often extremely technical, involving statistical analyses. This is known as quantitative analysis—analysis involving numbers. Often, the scientific method in the social sciences involves turning social life into something that can be measured numerically. It sounds rather odd, but there is logic to it. We strongly encourage you to eventually take a course in statistics—especially if you plan to continue in the social sciences. Indeed, this may be a requirement!

This data analysis section may also be qualitative. In this case, the analysis is conducted using data that is expressed as words, pictures, or objects. This may be more understandable for many students. This type of analysis is often used by anthropologists and historians, but you may find it useful in other social sciences disciplines, such as sociology or psychology. It is also likely that any given study will use a combination of quantitative and qualitative data. In any case, there is a series of strict guidelines that are established within each discipline for determining the most appropriate data collection and analysis procedures for scientific research.

For your purposes in writing a social sciences research paper, your instructors will most likely not expect you to comprehend all the procedures, especially if you have not taken a research methods, statistics, or other type of data collection and analysis course. You can make a cursory read through the data analysis section and move on to the next section, usually referred to as the discussion or conclusion sections.

The discussion and conclusion sections interpret the data analysis. These sections are very beneficial to you, as they discuss the results of the study as interpreted by the author(s). The discussion section will make the most sense if you understand the foundation and the methodology sections. If you wish to enhance your understanding of the methods of science, refer to a book on research methods in the social sciences. Each discipline focuses on a different aspect of social behavior; therefore, each discipline uses methods that are applicable to that field. Keep this in mind when looking for an appropriate research methods book to use as a resource.

USING SCHOLARLY BOOKS

You may want to use scholarly books (print as well as e-books) as secondary sources. If a book is written by a recognized authority or authorities, and if there is a reference section or bibliography at the end of the book, then you can be assured that it is a legitimate, scholarly source. While you will most heavily emphasize your primary, professional journal sources, some books can provide a useful overview of a great deal of theorizing and research findings.

Always read the preface and introduction to a book, as these will give you a good framework for mentally organizing the material that follows in the rest of the text. Educators sometimes refer to this as setting up a schema or mental diagram beforehand. Many educators have argued that having a schema will provide an overall sense of perspective and will make it much easier to comprehend and retain information.

Even if you are technically focusing on only one chapter in a scholarly book, you may want to leaf through or skim the rest of the book. You may be surprised at the useful and relevant information, data, graphics, and so on that a relatively quick perusal can give you.

TAKING NOTES

In your paper, you will often refer to the work of others. You should include as detailed a discussion as is relevant in your paper. Therefore, you should take notes on each of the articles, books, and other sources of information that you read. Some general questions you should try to answer for each source you read include:

- Who is the author(s)?
- What is the author(s) interested in? What is the research question? (The information you are reading may not contain a specific research question. If not, try to figure out what it might be.)
- Why does the author(s) think this research is important? What gap does it fill?
- Does the author(s) refer to any specific theory that is helping to guide his or her thinking about this question? If yes, what is it?
- Is the author(s) testing a specific hypothesis? If yes, what is it?
- What method is the researcher(s) using to collect data? Participant observation? Survey research? Experimentation? A combination of some or all of these? Be as specific as possible (e.g., the researcher conducted a survey using an open-ended interview schedule).
- What is the sample that the author(s) is gathering data about? For example, is it a sample of those in dating relationships for less than five years?
- How many people are included in the sample? This is typically written as $N = x$, where N is the number of people in the sample. For example, a sample size could be $N = 1500$ people who have dated the same person for less than five years.

- How is the data analysis conducted? Is it quantitative, or qualitative, or both? This section might be difficult. Do the best that you can.
- What interpretation does the author(s) give regarding the data analysis? What conclusions are drawn? If there is a hypothesis being tested, is it supported? Explain and elaborate.

In addition to answering these questions, be sure to write down (or cut and paste from an online source) all the reference or bibliographic information: author(s), year published, title of the article, journal title, volume number, issue number, and pages. Also, if you found the article online, jot down the Internet (URL) address and the date that you accessed the information. You should record all of the citation information for all types of sources, not only journal articles. In addition, you should write down as much information as possible from every source relevant to your paper. If you note a particular quote from a source, write down the page number(s) where it appears. Do not wait until you start the process of actually writing your paper to try and remember these things. Refer to Chapter 7 for more information.

There are many ways to take notes on the information that you read. A very traditional method is to use index cards (you can purchase these in packets of 100 to 200 cards) and keep a file (an old tissue box will do) to order the cards in. Jot down citation information, important points, pieces of data you may want to report on, and direct quotes that you might want to use in the paper. These cards will be useful later for helping you remember what you have read and for outlining your research paper. Other options include taking notes in word processing software (e.g., Microsoft Word) and creating files for each source. Alternatively, you can use reference management software such as EndNote, Mendeley, and RefWorks. In fact, there are currently over twenty different types of reference management software available! Some are free, some you must purchase, and some are subscription based. Each offers different functionalities, such as automatically capturing citation information from various databases that you search, exporting and importing files, and the ability to take notes as well as change citation format type to APA, Chicago, Harvard, Turabian, and MLA styles. Some people are very comfortable using reference management software to track citations, while others prefer the traditional way of recording on index cards. In any case, develop a method of managing the resources that you use so that these are easily accessible.

Having your notes and citation information handy is essential in the writing process. It is truly a time-saving device that will lead you to a more organized and better cited paper. There is nothing more time consuming or frustrating than searching through electronic files for a quote you know is there, but you just cannot find it! Unfortunately, when this happens, you must abide by this rule: If you cannot cite the source, you cannot use the information.

7

The APA Format

Writing and the Use of an Appropriate Format

Adhering to a specific format and style for a research paper is important. Using an accepted, organized standard style or format is imperative in writing a paper that will clearly and effectively make its point. Standardized citation formats also enable the reader to locate the information that you used to write up your research as well as to give attribution to the authors of the material you used. Later on in your professional career, you will also find that using the correct format is a minimum standard for publication purposes.

The two most well-known formats are the Modern Language Association (MLA) format that is used in the humanities disciplines, and the American Psychological Association (APA) format, formally known as the *Publication Manual of the American Psychological Association*, used in most social sciences disciplines. Another common format used by publishing houses is the *Chicago Manual of Style* (or Chicago style), and there may be additional formats for specific subject areas. Check with your professor or a librarian if you must follow a different format.

THE APA FORMAT

The APA format is one of the many styles used for citing and referencing sources. APA is a well-recognized method used in the social sciences. Unless you are requested to do otherwise, we encourage you to use this method for your own papers. While we are providing an overview of this method, academic libraries typically provide online access to official publications that explain this format in detail, and may also have print copies available for use. In addition, you can search for information about this style on the APA style website (http://apastyle.org). The examples used here are from the example paper found in Appendix B of this book. The location of the example is in parentheses for easy reference. At the time this book was revised, the most recent APA manual available is the sixth edition, second printing. This is the version of the APA manual used for the example paper.

Basic APA Format

According to the Purdue Online Writing Lab, a leading authority on APA format (https://owl.english.purdue.edu/owl/resource/560/01/), there are some basics you should know regarding the general format of APA, including general APA guidelines and the major sections of a paper that follows APA format (i.e., the title page, the abstract, the main body of the paper, and the reference list).

APA Title Page

APA requires that you have a title page to your paper that follows a specific format. The title page (which is the cover page to your paper) needs to include a title, the name of the author(s), and the institutional affiliation(s) of the author(s).

Using an 8.5" × 11" template on a word processing program, set margins at one inch on all sides of the template. Select a font that is easily readable, such as Times New Roman font, 12-point type. At the top of the page, left side, type: Running head: followed by the title of your paper in all capital letters. Since this is the first page of your paper, add the number 1 on the same line as the running head, at the top right of the page.

In the center of the title page, type your title in capital and small letters, followed by the name(s) of the author(s) of the paper (in this case you would add your name), followed by the author(s) affiliation (use the name of the college or university where you conducted your research). This information should be centered on the page and double-spaced. Here is an example title page for the sample paper found in Appendix B:

Running head: IS VIOLENCE IN DATING RELATIONSHIPS CONCEPTU-

ALLY DISTINCT FROM VIOLENCE IN MARITAL RELATIONSHIPS?

Is Violence in Dating Relationships Conceptually Distinct

From Violence In Marital Relationships?

Mia Smith

University of Central Missouri

Your professor may ask you to add additional information, such as the name of the course and the date. This information is not a part of APA format, but the professor may find it useful to identify who wrote the paper, for what course, and when.

APA Abstract

The abstract begins on the second page of your paper. At the top of the page you should already have your page header. This is the title of your paper typed in all capitalized letters and followed by the number 2 for the second page of your paper. The abstract is also double-spaced using the same font as the title page. (You should use the same font throughout the entire paper.) Center the word "abstract" two spaces below the page header, double-space and start your abstract on the left-hand side of the margin. Do not indent the first line.

An abstract is a brief summary of the research described in detail in the paper and is typically about 250 to 500 words in length. In the abstract include the purpose of your research, the question(s) you address, the type of research you conducted (such as quantitative—statistical analysis, and/or qualitative—open-ended survey questions) if applicable, the results of your research, and recommendations for future research on this topic—again, if applicable. Here is an example abstract for the sample paper found in Appendix B:

Abstract

This research examines the physical violence in dating relationships, specifically addressing the question: Is violence in dating relationships conceptually distinct from violence in marital relationships? The following factors are taken into consideration. First, dating violence is described as a form of family violence or, more precisely, intimate violence. Second, the role of dating and courtship must be taken into account. Third, dating violence is recognized as being distinct yet on a continuum of other forms of violence. In general, this study found research on dating violence is studied as a distinct phenomenon but is increasingly examined in the broader context of intimate violence.

Citing Following APA Format

There are specific standards to follow in order to cite the sources that you use in your paper according to APA format. The type of source you are citing determines the format that you will follow. For example, different formats are used to cite a work by one author, a work by several authors, citing a part(s) of a source, and citing information found in electronic form. Below are the more common citation formats used in research papers. For additional citation formats, refer to the 2009 *Publication Manual of the American Psychology Association* (6th ed.).

Reference Citations in Text

In addition to the reference list you will develop and put at the end of your paper, you may also refer to specific experts or studies within the paper itself. APA refers to this type of citation as "in-text" citation. In-text citations document the sources you referred to when writing your paper. Unless referring to a specific quote in a work or a specific section, you will begin your in-text citation by citing the author(s) and date of the source. For the most part, the author(s) will be a) the author(s) of a book, b) the author(s) of a chapter of a book, c) the author(s) of a journal article, or d) the author(s) of an electronic reference.

In citing books, it is important to distinguish between books with one or multiple authors and books that are edited and have one or multiple authors per chapter. If the book has one or several authors, this is whom you cite. Thus, if you use information from three chapters of a book that has one or multiple authors, you will be citing one source. If you use information from three chapters of a book with one or multiple *chapter* authors, you will be citing three sources, and these are then referenced according to chapter author(s) on the reference list page.

Citing One Work by One Author

APA format uses the author-date method of citation. Use the last name of the author only (do not include suffixes such as Jr.) and the year of the publication. These are inserted in the text at the appropriate point:

What was once thought of as a rare occurrence between family members (Gelles, 1980)

is now recognized as a common, often socially accepted phenomenon in many, if not

all, types of intimate relationships. (Appendix B, paragraph 7)

James Makepeace (1981) was the first to suggest that social scientists examine courtship

violence as a link between violence experienced in childhood and later violence experi-

enced in marriage. (Appendix B, paragraph 7)

Citing One Work by Two Authors

When a work has two authors, always cite both authors' names every time the reference occurs in the text.

In 1985, the second national survey of family violence was conducted by the Family

Violence Research Laboratory at the University of New Hampshire (Straus & Gelles,

1990). (Appendix B, paragraph 2)

Straus and Gelles (1990) found in the 1985 National Family Violence Survey that about

161 couples per 1,000 couples experienced one or more physical assaults on a partner

during that year, and that 34/1,000 wives were severely assaulted (1.8 million) by their

husbands. (Appendix B, paragraph 3)

Citing One Work by Three to Five Authors

When a work has three, four, or five authors, cite all authors the first time the
reference occurs. In additional citations of these authors, include only the first author
followed by et al. (meaning "and others") and the year. Note that "et" is not followed
by a period.

Current studies of dating violence among high school students, for example, by James,

West, Deters, and Armijo (2000) found rates of 19% to 59% had been the victim of

physical violence. James et al. (2000) studied psychological and physical abuse in a

sample of adolescents. (Appendix B, paragraph 9)

Citing a Work by Six or More Authors

Cite only the last name of the first author followed by et al. every time it is used.

Citing a Work by an Organization

If the author of a work is a specific organization, treat the name of the organization as the author of the work.

The United States Department of Health and Human Services (2017) indicates . . .

Citing Personal Communications

If you want to cite information from interviews that you have conducted, email
exchanges, or other forms of communication, indicate that the information is from

personal communication. Do not include personal communications in your reference list.

(J. Stern, personal communication, August 12, 2018).

Citing Information from Multiple Sources

Many times you will discover that researchers may state similar findings or make similar arguments. Rather than go through each one individually, you may want to summarize the work of more than one source in the same sentence or the same paragraph.

This is most clear in efforts to understand violence within gay and lesbian relationships

(Letellier, 1994; Lobel, 1986; Renzetti, 1994). (Appendix B, paragraph 4)

The Reference List

The reference list at the end of your paper provides all of the material needed to retrieve each source cited in the text. Remember: If it was cited in the text, it must be fully referenced in the reference list. Refer to the reference list in Appendix B for examples.

The sources should be listed alphabetically by the surname of the first author. When referencing several works by one author, they should be arranged by year of publication, with the earliest year first. One-author entries precede multiple-author entries beginning with the same surname. References with the same first author and different second or third authors and so on are arranged alphabetically by the surname of the second or third authors, and so on.

Authors may also be an agency, association, or institution, or occasionally there will be no author at all. In the first case, alphabetize by the agency, association, or institution. If there is no author, the title moves to the author position. Only use the word "anonymous" as an author if the source states that the author is anonymous.

Following are examples from books, chapters in books, journal articles, and electronic sources. For each one, note the hanging indentation following the first line; the use of upper- and lowercase letters; the position of periods, commas, colons, and spacing; use of italics; and the ampersand symbol (&) in place of the word "and."

Referencing books with one or multiple authors requires the following:

- Author(s): First and middle initials (if available) and full surname
- Year of publication
- Title of book
- City of publication
- Publishing company

Lobel, K. (Ed.). (1986). *Naming the violence: Speaking out about lesbian battering.* Seattle,

WA: Seal Press.

Author: K. Lobel
Year of publication: 1986
Title of book: *Naming the violence: Speaking out about lesbian battering*
City of publication: Seattle, WA
Publishing company: The Seal Press

Referencing chapters in books (the chapters have different authors and the book is edited) requires the following:

- Author(s) of chapter
- Year of publication
- Title of chapter
- Editor(s) of book
- Title of book
- Page numbers of chapter
- City of publication
- Publishing company

Stets, J. E., & Straus, M. A. (1990). The marriage license as a hitting license: A com-

parison of assaults in dating, cohabitating, and married couples. In M. A. Straus &

R. J. Gelles (Eds.), *Physical violence in American families: Risk factors and adaptations*

to violence in 8,145 families (pp. 227-244). New Brunswick, NJ: Transaction Books.

Authors of chapter: J. E. Stets and M. A. Straus
Year of publication: 1990
Title of chapter: The marriage license as a hitting license: A comparison
                           of assaults in dating, cohabitating, and married couples.
Editors of book: J. E. Stets and R. J. Gelles
Title of book: *Physical violence in American families: Risk factors and*
                           adaptations to violence in 8,145 families.
Page numbers of chapter: pp. 227–244
City of publication: New Brunswick, NJ
Publishing company: Transaction Books

Citing Information from Electronic Sources

This part of the APA manual has been significantly expanded and includes various ways to cite information found in electronic format. The list is too long to reproduce here. If you want to cite information from an electronic source that is not explained below, please refer to the sixth edition of the *APA Manual.*

Citing an Article from an Online Periodical

Cite articles retrieved from online periodicals the same way that you would cite an article from a periodical that is printed, and add the URL.

Author, B. C., & Author, D. E. (Date of publication). Title of the article. *Title of the*

Online Periodical, volume number (issue number if provided). Retrieved from http://

www.url.edu/complete/restofurl/

Westenberg, L. (2017). When she calls for help: Domestic violence in Christian families.

Social Sciences, 6(3). Retrieved from http://www.mdpi.com/2076-0760/6/3/71

Citing an Article from a Database

Cite an article retrieved from a database like you would an article from a print source. The reasoning behind this type of citing is that, should the reader not have access to the online database, they can find it in print.

Cho, H., & Huang, L. (2017). Aspects of help seeking among collegiate victims of

dating violence. *Journal of Family Violence, 32*(4), 409-417. Retrieved from http://

web.b.ebscohost.com/

You will come across still other sources that are not illustrated here in both paper and electronic formats. For example, paper formats include newspaper articles, brochures, classic works, manuscripts, and personal communications. Other electronic formats include blog posts, podcasts, social media posts, online videos, and other Internet resources. In such instances, consult the most recent edition of the *Publication of the American Psychological Association* or the American Psychological Association style website at http://apastyle.org.

Please take a moment to complete Worksheet 7: Chapters in Books, which appears in Appendix C.

8

The Writing Process Itself

You Can't Edit a Blank Page

At some point in your research and writing, remember that you can't edit a blank page. What we mean is, begin! If you commit something to writing, you then have something to work with. Alternatively, if you obsess for weeks about how and where to begin, you will most likely procrastinate until you no longer have enough time to do a good job on the research paper. We have found that the best technique for writing is constructing an outline and then sitting at the word processor, "filling in" the outline with a running stream of consciousness—your thoughts and findings on each of the outline subtopics. This is analogous to a brainstorming process. Try to write at least one page each day this way. In a few weeks, you will have a draft of your paper written. Going back later and editing, correcting, adding, and modifying will be much easier once you have this body of writing to work with.

Remember to clearly distinguish your own theorizing and findings from other sources that you have read. The reader must be able to tell at any particular point whether you are speaking for yourself or for others in the field. You cannot simply mass information together and present conclusions in your research paper without properly crediting each source. On the undergraduate level, and certainly on the graduate level, such a paper will be returned with a very low grade indeed.

When summarizing others' theories and findings, be sure to identify the main points and condense these without losing their meaning. To whatever degree possible, paraphrase. Use your own words to describe what the original author(s) was trying to say. If there is a phrase that you cannot put in your own words, be sure to put it within quotation marks and, of course, cite the original source with page number(s).

While it is important to use a great deal of documentation from the literature that you have reviewed, and while you should cite every source, your paper should not be a kind of patchwork quilt with many patches and little quilting. Stringing together

51

excerpts from someone else's writing and theorizing, even if properly cited, with little or no material of your own will result in a very poor, non-scholarly paper.

You may understand what literal plagiarism is—quoting directly from a source without citing where the information came from—but you also need to be aware of conceptual plagiarism. Conceptual plagiarism occurs when a writer presents some-one else's original theories without crediting the source. In other words, if you write about the ego, the id, and the superego without alluding to Sigmund Freud as the originator of these concepts, you are engaging in conceptual plagiarism. While you will want to cite sources, and use some excerpts directly from the readings you have reviewed, you must do this intelligently. Lifting entire sections off of the Internet, for example, even if one has properly cited them, is little more than thinly disguised plagiarism. Note that professors can easily use such tools as Turnitin and iThenticate to verify that the content of your research paper is, in fact, original and that you did not plagiarize from another source.

Remember also that, if you understand very little about the theories or method-ology in a particular article, or do not understand anything at all, you should not include that article in your literature review. Reporting on the article conveys the tacit assumption that you have understood its contents. Especially in upper-level undergraduate courses and in graduate school, orally defending research that includes content that you do not fully understand in front of an individual or a committee can lead to a great deal of embarrassment (at best) and possibly a failing grade (at worst).

When you finally have your paper written, be sure to proofread it manually, as well as conducting a spell check. Remember that a spell check program will only find absolute misspellings. It may not detect incorrect grammar, errors in tenses, misspelled names of authors, and so on.

SHOULD WRITERS EXPRESS THEIR OWN OPINIONS?

Students will notice that the writing in much of what they read, even articles in a professional journal, seems to have a particular opinion or "bent" on their topic. Sometimes students ask if all scholarly writing should not be absolutely objective. "Absolute objectivity" is an ideal that has rarely, if ever, been seen in practice. For any social scientist to claim that he or she approaches a topic with no preconceptions, no previously held beliefs, and no prejudices, is disingenuous. We have all lived in a world and formed a belief system. To assume that this will not influence our scien-tific research is to be less than candid with ourselves. The most interesting writings are those that are forthright in stating their points of view.

What differentiates scientific writing from opinion papers, however, is substantiat-ing, with research and data, your point of view, and being willing to admit that your hypothesis has little support. Only if the writer feels passionately about a subject can the reader be expected to become enthused about a book or article.

SOME TIPS ON WRITING PAPERS
AND SOME FREQUENT PITFALLS TO AVOID

1. *Do not use sexist language.* Instead of using the generic *he* or *she*, use sexually neutral language, such as *(s)he* or *his/her* or *his or her*. Students often argue that this will sound awkward or stilted. This kind of writing rarely sounds awkward or stilted, and, as more and more of the academic (and even popularized) literature is now written in this style, readers are becoming used to this phrasing. Be on your guard for sexist language where you might least expect it to crop up. For example, use the term *humankind* instead of *mankind* or *personnel* instead of *manpower*. You may also write in the plural third person (*they, their, them*).

2. *Do not use racist or ageist terms.* Once again, these terms may crop up more readily than you might imagine, and you must be vigilant. For example, when recently attending a workshop hosted by an academic, the presenter argued that, at his university, the administration wanted the faculty members to be "good little Indians." It took a great deal of persuading to convince this individual that he was indeed using racist language. Please also note that it is appropriate to refer to individuals under eighteen years of age as *boys* or *girls* or *young men* or *young women*. Individuals over eighteen years of age are referred to as *men* or *women*.

3. *Don't change verb tenses gratuitously.* Many writers shift back and forth between present tense and past tense. Writing in this way is both distracting and confusing.

4. *Always place modifying words as closely as possible to those words being modified.* Do not write, for example, "The president, who gave a speech in the pouring rain, out in the field in the middle of the afternoon, was profound." Rather, you might write, "The president was profound in his speech given in the pouring rain in the middle of the afternoon."

5. *Always write complete sentences.* Do not write informally and in the form of an outline. Many students write exactly as they would speak or text, that is, informally. This is not scholarly form and is truly unacceptable in a college-level paper. For your finished paper, phrases and shorthand are not acceptable at all.

6. *Do not use unnecessary commas, colons, and semicolons.* Students often think that, when in doubt, use punctuation. Actually in this case, less is more. You should be sure that you are appropriately using any such punctuation.

Writers will look at a blank sheet of paper or the computer screen and wonder how it will be when their work is done. They often look at that sheet of paper or computer screen for a very long time! Writing well does take time, in addition to requiring a great deal of practice and hard work. Not only should your papers read well, they should look good too. When reading the literature, we suggest that you read with a writer's eye—recognize the writing style of the work; and when writing your paper, write with a reader's eye—think about how well your readers will follow and understand your work.

College campuses have writing centers available to students. Writing centers are places where students can go for help or simply work quietly, knowing that assistance is nearby if needed. Questions may come up throughout the writing process. Mentors are often available to guide students through any aspect of the writing exercise, from understanding the assignment through reading final drafts. Students should never expect mentors to grade their papers, nor should they expect mentors to be their editors. However, mentors do serve to help students each step of the way. We strongly encourage you to visit your campus writing center.

Professors are also available to help guide your work. If you are having difficulty at any point, seek out the professor. As always, it is best to come prepared to a meeting with your professor. Try not to be intimidated by professors; after all, they have been where you are now, and they want their students to do well.

You should begin the literature gathering, note taking, and organizing process early so that you have ample time to write the paper. Putting a paper together is a constant work in progress. At some point you need to begin the writing process; at some point you must decide, "This is the final version!" Do your best to make the reader want to read your paper.

9

Presenting Your Research

As part of your research assignment, you may be required to give a presentation. Students are often frightened of this because it involves standing and speaking before a group of people. Presenters who know their material and who have organized that material in a meaningful way are more likely to give interesting presentations to their fellow classmates and others. If you are giving a presentation, then you should be prepared! A presentation is usually a somewhat simplified version of a more complex paper. You should do your best not to read a paper. However, you should have notes to follow and to guide you. In all cases, you should follow an outline. The guidelines for creating an outline are found in Chapter 5. Follow those steps in preparing your presentation.

Know your material! This is very important. While you may not refer to everything you know on your subject, knowledge allows you to confidently create a solid presentation. In addition, you may be asked questions that had not been addressed in the presentation. As someone who is expected to be familiar with a topic, you should be ready to answer many questions.

ENHANCING YOUR PRESENTATION: USING TECHNOLOGY

It is common practice to use some type of visual aid with your presentation. By the time this book is published, it is possible that new technologies will be available for you to use to enhance your presentation. The rule of thumb here is to keep it simple! Be very comfortable and familiar with any technology you select to use. Nothing is more frustrating than relying on technology for the bulk of your presentation, only to discover that it does not work as you intended. Too often, presenters (novice through experienced) are ready to do their presentation on campus or elsewhere, only to find out that they do not have the correct cable to connect to their laptop, the wi-fi doesn't work, the digital projector is not compatible with the technology you are using, or the electricity and Internet access are completely unavailable. Of course, you want to avoid these situations at all costs, but issues do arise unexpectedly and you need to be prepared to handle them. In this regard, it is strongly suggested that, at minimum, you bring the text of your presentation (e.g., your outline, your notes) in paper format. This way the show can go on if the technology fails.

Types of Presentation Technologies

There are a multitude of presentation technologies available today. Probably the most common is the use of PowerPoint presentations. However, presenters also use web pages, other presentation software such as Prezi, even embedding video within a poster presentation! The options are endless, but be practical—individuals are coming to hear from you about your research, not to be entertained with flashy visuals. In this regard, use technology sparingly. Your visuals should not distract attention away from the subject matter. Use visuals only to the extent that they enable you to convey information more effectively to your audience. Concentrate on the content of your presentation. Again, the audience is interested in learning from you; you are not there to show that you have mastered this technology.

Some presentation technologies that you can use to make your presentation more interesting are presented here.

Visual Viewers

Sometimes called an ELMO Visualizer, WolfVision Visualizer, or document camera, a visual viewer is a piece of equipment that allows you to place any object on its platform and display it on a screen. The object can be a book, a page of text, even a three-dimensional object. The viewer displays the object as it actually exists. Using a visual viewer can be very effective when showing an audience a section of text from a rare book, the prototype of an item, a manuscript, and so on. Most viewers can allow you to enlarge the image. Not all classrooms and other presentation venues are equipped with visual viewers. You may need to find out if one is available for you to use.

Web Pages

Creating a web page or even a simple website is very easy to do. The advantages of using a web page in your presentation is that you can access Internet sites that you may want to show your audience, as well as make your site available for your audience to access via the Internet after your presentation. Web pages provide you with much flexibility. You can create a PowerPoint presentation, provide links to quality websites, add sound, and even use video streaming for a complete multimedia experience. Many students now create websites on specific topics, make them available on the web, and then add the Internet address of the website to their résumé so that potential employers can gain insight into the quality of the work they can create. There are many free sites on the Internet that you can use to create your own website, such as Wix, Site123, and hibu.

If you decide to develop a web page or website for your presentation, you will need to make sure that the room you are using for your presentation has the technology (e.g., computer with appropriate software; digital projector, monitor, or screen; speakers for sound) compatible with what you have used to develop your presentation. You will also need Internet access to access your website or other links found on the Internet. It is a good idea to post your website on the Internet at least a few days prior to your presentation to make sure that it is accessible.

Using Apps and Other Resources to Engage Your Audience

In your presentation, you may have time to further engage your audience by using apps and other types of resources. Below are some examples that you can use. (Remember to test these out before your presentation.)

Polling Websites

Polling is an easy way to get a sense of what your audience knows about your topic, as well as what areas within your presentation they are most interested in learning about. Using smartphone technology, you can ask your audience to answer a question or respond to a statement in real time. A polling website will receive, then automatically post the results that are viewable on the display technology you are using (such as a digital projector and screen, or monitor). Students not only use polling websites in their presentations, but instructors use polling websites as a way to interact with students. Some of the more popular polling websites are Poll Everywhere, Kahoot, and PollDaddy.

Multi-Engagement Apps

Newer apps coming onto the market (many for free) not only allow for polling your audience, but also allow you to easily share your unique URL, view and download your slides from your presentation, jot down notes, share on social media, and provide feedback, all in real time. Glisser is one such app available for Android and iOS.

Hearing Your Audience

One of these most challenging components of a presentation, especially with a large audience, is being able to hear and respond to audience questions and comments. Traditionally, microphones would be placed on stands throughout the venue for audience members to walk to and talk into the microphone. The presenter would then respond from the stage using his or her own microphone. Crowd Mics now allow anyone to use their smartphone as a microphone! All the individual needs to do is enable Crowd Mic on their phone and they have a mic. Crowd Mic also provides for real-time polling and is available for Android and iOS.

Communicating Your Message Effectively

Below are some tips to help you effectively present your research. These are best practices proven to help make your presentation dynamic and interesting.

The Revealing Technique

We have found that one of the most effective ways to communicate information to an audience is to present no more than three or four statements or pieces of data or information at the same time. A good rule is to use the "revealing" technique of presenting information to your audience. To do this, divide each of the pages or screens you are using into thirds. Present your data on the first third, covering the second and third portions; continuing by revealing the second portion, and then the third, until the entire screen is visible to the audience. Presenting all the information at once may overwhelm and confuse your audience. By revealing your information systematically, you keep your audience focused on the topic you are discussing.

Use Large Font

Another very effective technique is to use a large enough font size so that individuals located at the back or sides of a classroom or other presentation space can read the information you are presenting. Keep in mind that text, images, charts, and graphs need to be viewed by the entire audience, no matter where they are sitting in the room. During your practice rehearsal, sit in different locations of the room to see if you can view your presentation. For example, the text and images may be large enough to view, but if you place these toward the bottom of the screen, those sitting in the back or along the sides of the room may not be able to see these. If you cannot see all of the information on each screen, then you will need to adjust your text and images accordingly.

Use Color

When developing your digital presentation, consider using two or more colors to delineate topics, text, columns in a graph, or different threads of thought. Presentation software provides hundreds of colors in addition to being able to highlight text and colors to diminish the text you are currently not talking about. Like checking font size and visibility of your presentation from all angles in a room, pay attention to the colors you use and ask yourself: Is that color effective? Can it be clearly seen? Am I using one color to highlight a part of my presentation, and other color to indicate a different part? Yellows, white text on a black background, and very light hues of all kinds of color are challenging to see. If you prefer a certain color, but it is not readily visible, you can always bold or underline words in that color.

Preplanning is strongly advised if you decide to use technology for your presentation. If you are presenting for a class, check with your professor or computer center on campus to determine the availability of the technology you need in the location you are presenting. This should be done at least three to four weeks in advance of your presentation. You will also want to practice your presentation at least once in the room that you will be using. This way, you can become familiar with any equipment, lighting, or other changes you will need to make, and you will be assured that your program runs on the equipment provided. Do not count on developing your presentation at home and then using it successfully on campus without practicing. The technology on campus may not be compatible with the technology you use at home. It may seem like a waste of time, but there have been hundreds of instances where students are scheduled to do their presentation, only to discover that the technology does not work or is incompatible with their own technology. Doing a rehearsal or dry run is essential.

When you are practicing your presentation, it also is a good idea to record yourself or have a friend do it for you. Using a smartphone, set up the phone so that it captures you doing your presentation and record. It's that easy! Then you can review your presentation and make improvements as needed. There are also apps available to give you guidance, help you with your speech patterns, timing, and more. Some campuses also have centers for teaching and learning with staff who are able to review your recorded presentation and make suggestions for improvement. Do not be shy! This is your time to work on your people skills, and a campus is a safe, supportive environment in which to do this.

POSTER SESSIONS

Another way that professionals share information, particularly at conferences, is by participating in poster sessions. A poster session is simply a time set aside at a conference for conference participants to share their latest research. Poster session participants (researchers) literally bring a poster that illustrates their research. The posters are all displayed on tables in a large venue, and conference attendees can freely visit each poster to learn about current research. A specific time may be scheduled at the conference to allow the poster presenters to stand next to their poster in order to answer questions. Otherwise, the posters are available for viewing throughout the conference.

Most times conference organizers will put out a "call for posters" several months (sometimes a year) prior to the conference date. Once submitted, a poster may be peer-reviewed before it is officially accepted. If the conference publishes conference proceedings, typically a synopsis of the poster sessions that appear at the conference will be included along with papers and other presentations.

Creating a poster for a poster session is fairly easy, but does require some planning. You will need to communicate the key points of your research on the poster through text and graphics. Typically, a poster measures 48" × 36" in a horizontal layout. It is recommended that the size of text on a poster needs to be readable from about three feet away. A good rule of thumb is to use a 60-point font for the title and headings, a 30-point font for headings and text, and no less than 18 points elsewhere. It is also recommended that you use Arial, Helvetica, or other sans-serif fonts for titles and headings.

New technology also enables your flat, two-dimensional poster to come to life! HP Reveal is an app that you can download to your smartphone to embed video "onto" your poster. Adding a technology hot spot on your poster allows anyone with a smart device to hold it up to your poster, find the hot spot, and click—revealing whatever you recorded to add to your poster! You can record a brief overview of your project as well as other interesting aspects of your research. Recordings/videos should be brief—no more than two minutes long. This is just a way to communicate your research results to the audience in a different way.

Most colleges and universities have a poster template that you can download from their website along with guidelines and suggestions for creating an effective poster. Generally speaking, best practices in poster design (in addition to font and point size) include using a short, catchy, but descriptive title; listing the research investigators and their affiliations; acknowledging the agencies who provided funding for the research; and highlighting the key points and/or outcomes of your research. If you are submitting your poster for a conference, inquire if there are specific guidelines in terms of size or format for poster submissions. Today, posters can be printed on heavy stock paper (glossy or non-glossy) as well as on light fabric, the latter of which allows you to fold up your poster and pack it in your carry-on luggage. Ask if you will need to bring something on which to mount the poster (such as foam board) or if these will be provided. If provided, make sure that you bring thumbtacks with you so that you can attach your poster.

Creating an effective poster takes time and planning. You may need to work through several iterations before you complete the final version. Ask your professors and graduate students for advice. Planning ahead will help you to confidently put together a poster that you can be proud of!

PROFESSIONAL PRESENTATIONS

As you have learned through this chapter, technologies and other strategies are available for you to use to develop presentations and posters explaining your research. You can create pie charts, bar graphs, and even more advanced visuals fairly easily. There are numerous options available to you, with more becoming available every day. An eye-catching presentation along with audience interaction will enable individuals to retain the information you present.

It would be nice if giving a presentation were not a high-anxiety-producing event, as it is for many students (and even for professionals). However, the more concerned about presentations you are, the more likely you will be prepared. Keep in mind that your classmates and others are learning something from you. Know the material, have guidelines to follow, perhaps enhance the presentation with technology, and be proud of your work. Throughout our lives we find that we must give presentations of one sort or another. There is no time like the present to begin!

Turn to Worksheet 11: Presentation (in Appendix C) and complete the questions.

10

Some Final Thoughts

A well-organized, well-written, and well-presented research paper or project may seem overwhelming for most students at the beginning of the creative process. This manual provides step-by-step guidelines for students in the social sciences. The process should become less burdensome, if it is indeed a burden, with each completed paper or project.

It should be clear by now that the process is quite tangible and explicit. Developing a research question is the crucial first step. Finding available material related to the question requires both information search skills and a critical analysis of the literature. The library (both the physical building and the virtual, online version) is the main source of quality information. Once the material is sorted through, an outline is developed and key points identified. At this point, it is extremely important to stay focused. Each key point in the outline must be expanded upon using the scholarly literature as the main source of information. In the final paper or project, sources must be properly cited. A complete reference list must be included.

While this all seems pro forma and routine, keep in mind that writing a research paper for the social sciences involves a great deal of abstract thought, reflection, critical thinking, organization, and technical skill. These skills range from reading the research to writing and presenting the findings. Students should use any other available resources beyond this manual to help if there is a need. These resources include instructors, librarians, and campus writing centers.

Finally, in addition to enhancing one's knowledge on a topic and receiving a good class grade, writing a skillful research paper and giving a successful presentation can be quite satisfying. The processes of scholarly research, writing, and presenting provide students with a number of skills for life, such as the ability to view the world more objectively, understand and evaluate problems, understand personal issues in a broader social context, organize thoughts and information, conceptualize difficulties clearly, and write well. Thus, we encourage you to persevere. It is well worth the effort!

Appendix A

Research Questions Posed by Prior Students

Among the wide range of questions that could be posed by social sciences under-graduate students, the following issues have been actually researched by students enrolled in college or university:

- Has education on AIDS in African American communities significantly helped to decrease the number of African Americans at risk for AIDS?
- What obstacles do young, single mothers and their children face?
- Are children from divorced families more prone to delinquent activities than children from intact families?
- What is the relationship between marital status and workforce participation for women?
- How does access to contraceptives affect the likelihood that teenagers use contraceptives?
- What is the relationship between socioeconomic factors and domestic violence?
- How does level of education affect men's and women's perceptions of gender roles?
- How has the rise in bias-motivated crime against homosexual Americans during the last thirty years led to the development of legislation to address the issue of hate crimes based on sexual orientation?
- What is the relationship between neighborhood level of interaction and incidence of crime?
- What is the effect of maternal employment on children's well-being?
- Is inner-city crime, especially that committed by young minority-group members, overrepresented in the media?
- Does the American news media depict youth violence in a fashion disproportionate to its coverage of violence as a whole?

- How does social support following an abusive childhood affect people's lives?
- How do women's work roles affect family life?
- How do grades in school influence deviance in later life?
- What factors influence people with terminal illnesses to choose euthanasia, specifically physician-assisted suicide?
- Does family structure affect a child's academic achievement?
- How do young women respond to the gender gap in wages?
- How do affirmative action policies, required by all companies, influence the hiring and placement of racial minority groups and women?
- How closely linked are socioeconomic status during childhood and socioeconomic status in adulthood?
- How do preventative programs affect juvenile delinquency?
- How does drug use during adolescence affect identity formation?
- What is the relationship between teen substance abuse and teen physical violence in dating relationships?
- Have the educational requirements of occupations risen over the last two decades in a way that is consistent with the rewards of those occupations?
- Why is there an overrepresentation of minority groups in the juvenile justice system?
- To what extent are women occupying executive-level management in the 500 (Fortune 500) public corporations?
- How does poverty affect children's success in school?
- Is there a difference in the number of cases of sexual aggression and sexual victimization for schools with and those without rape prevention or education programs?
- Does pornography influence negative attitudes toward women?
- How does after-school care affect adolescents' drinking and school performance?
- How does being in college influence drinking behavior?

Appendix B

Example Paper

Please note: The numbering of paragraphs in the following example paper is for instructional purposes only. Numbering paragraphs is not acceptable APA format. Do not number the paragraphs when writing your paper. Use a one-inch margin for all margins.

Double space the text of your paper. (For purposes of space, the example paper is shown single spaced.) Do not use excessively large or small font size. APA style recommends using a font that is easy to read, such as 12-point Times New Roman.

Your professor will provide instructions on how to turn in your paper. Some professors prefer that you submit a print copy of your paper, stapled in the left-hand corner. Others will accept your paper electronically. In all cases, back up your paper in electronic format and make a print copy for yourself.

Running head: IS VIOLENCE IN DATING RELATIONSHIPS CONCEPTU-
ALLY DISTINCT FROM VIOLENCE IN MARITAL RELATIONSHIPS?

Is Violence in Dating Relationships Conceptually Distinct
from Violence in Marital Relationships?
Mia Smith
University of Central Missouri

Abstract

This research examines the physical violence in dating relationships, specifically addressing the question: Is violence in dating relationships conceptually distinct from violence in marital relationships? The following factors are taken into consideration. First, dating violence is described as a form of family violence or, more precisely, intimate violence. Second, the role of dating and courtship must be taken into account. Third, dating violence is recognized as being distinct yet on a continuum of other forms of violence. In general, this study found research on dating violence is studied as a distinct phenomenon but is increasingly examined in the broader context of intimate violence.

Paragraph 1 The purpose of this paper is to examine physical violence in dating relationships. Specifically, this paper addresses the question: Is violence in dating relationships conceptually distinct from violence in marital relationships? The following factors are taken into consideration. First, dating violence is described as a form of family violence or, more precisely, intimate violence. Second, the role of dating and courtship must be taken into account. Third, dating violence is recognized as being distinct, yet on a continuum of other forms of violence.

Paragraph 2 Dating violence is a form of family violence. Research in the area of family violence has its beginnings in the late 1960s and early 1970s. In 1985, the second national survey of family violence was conducted by the Family Violence Research Laboratory at the University of New Hampshire (Straus & Gelles, 1990). The rate of violence against children was 23/1,000 (1.5 million children each year) when socially sanctioned acts of slapping or hitting with an object are omitted. It increased to 110/1,000 (6.9 million children each year) when all acts of violence were included.

Paragraph 3 Straus and Gelles (1990) found in the 1985 National Family Violence Survey that about 161 couples per 1,000 couples experienced one or more physical assaults on a partner during that year, and that 34/1,000 wives (1.8 million) were severely assaulted by their husbands. Severe assaults involved the most dangerous acts, such as punching, biting, kicking, and choking. The Family Violence Research Laboratory studies use the conflict tactics scale to measure the frequency of self-reported incidents of how persons deal with conflict in their relationships, from reasoning, threatening, or using force. The conflict tactics scale is used regularly in studies to determine frequency and occurrences of violence in relationships.

Paragraph 4 Researchers are now examining violence by women toward men. Early studies by Steinmetz (1977–1978) and Straus and Gelles (1990) showed that women were violent toward men. These studies received criticism in the family violence research world, particularly from feminist researchers who were focusing on women as victims and men as perpetrators as a result of inequality. For example, Irene Frieze (2000) explained that feminist researchers assumed that men were aggressors and women victims of marital violence. Other actors had to be considered as well to help understand violence in families and in other types of intimate relationships that do not limit the theoretical focus to male domination and female subordination (e.g., see Stets & Pirog-Good, 1989). This is most clear in efforts to understand violence within gay and lesbian relationships (Letellier, 1994; Lobel, 1986; Renzetti, 1994).

Paragraph 5 Research in the area of family violence increasingly shows that women can be, and are, violent toward men. Once again quoting Irene Frieze (2000), "for feminist researchers of battered wives, one of the most disconcerting findings of studies of dating violence was that young women were found to be at least as violent, if not more violent than, the young men they were dating" (p. 681).

Paragraph 6 In the United States, romantic love emerges in the context of dating. Dating is a form of mate selection that involves the least commitment between couples. Teenagers are learning how to deal with each other as well as adjusting to physical sexual maturity. This can be a traumatic period. Some people are afraid of intimacy because it makes them more vulnerable; for example, they do not want to be dependent on someone else or risk being hurt. Irene Frieze (2000) wrote a chronology of the research on family violence and stated about dating violence that "although researchers continued to study marital violence, other social scientists were investigating another form of male-female violence—dating violence. Researchers came to believe that a pattern of violence was often established before marriage, during the dating period" (p. 681). James, West, Deters, and Armijo (2000) argued that dating violence among adolescents is a serious health problem that needs to be addressed.

Paragraph 7 It is becoming increasingly evident that violence is not limited to persons who are related to each other either legally or biologically. What was once thought of as a rare occurrence between family members (Gelles, 1980) is now recognized as common, often socially accepted phenomenon in many, if not all, types of intimate relationships. James Makepeace (1981) was the first to suggest that social scientists examine courtship violence as a link between violence experienced in childhood and later violence experienced in marriage. Others suggested that relationship violence be examined regardless of marital status, because abuse in courtship resembles that which is reported in marriage (Roscoe & Benaske, 1985).

Paragraph 8 Makepeace (1981) initially hypothesized that abusive relationships would terminate for dating couples more quickly than in marital relationships because a couple's reasons for staying together in marriage did not seem to apply in a dating relationship. Twenty-one percent of the respondents in his college survey had at least one direct experience with courtship violence. The forms of violence most often sustained were pushing and slapping, while more severe forms of violence were sustained least often, such as punching, striking with an object, assaulting with a weapon, or choking. Contrary to his expectations, abusive relationships between dating partners did not result in relationship termination following physically violent arguments more quickly than between married partners. Other studies have found high percentages of physical violence in dating relationships. Early studies showed that 20% to 66% of couples experienced some form of violence (Laner & Thompson, 1982; McKinney, 1986; Pagelow, 1984). Those figures appear to be consistent with more recent research (Frieze, 2005).

Paragraph 9 Henton, Cate, Koval, Lloyd, and Christopher (1983) carried out the first study of dating violence among high school youth. They found that 12% of high school students had experienced violence in dating relationships. Current studies of dating violence among high school students, for example, by James et al. (2000), found that 19% to 59% had been victims of physical violence. James et al. (2000) studied psychological and physical abuse in a sample of adolescents. Their findings reinforced that at least 25% of adolescents experience psychological and physical abuse in their relationships. They defined youth violence in dating relationships as a serious public health problem that needs to be addressed.

Paragraph 10 Another study carried out by Howard and Wang (2003) used survey data from the 1999 Youth Risk Behavior Survey to identify risk profiles of adolescent girls who were victims of dating violence. The survey sample was a representative sample of ninth- through twelfth-grade U.S. females (N = 7,824). They found that almost one in ten girls reported being a victim of physical dating violence within the past year. Researchers are examining dating violence and its relationship to high-risk behaviors, such as substance abuse, feelings of sadness or hopelessness, and thoughts of suicide.

Paragraph 11 The research on dating violence is being used in ways to help stop the violence and protect victims of violence. With access to electronic information readily available, prevention programs are easily accessible. A Google search using the key words *dating violence* retrieved over 21 million results (Google search, 2018). The information on dating violence is often a part of a larger website addressing domestic violence or crime victimization. For instance, the Alabama Coalition Against Domestic Violence (ACADV, n.d.) is a "nonprofit organization dedicated to working toward a peaceful society where domestic violence no longer exists" (para. 1). The categories linked on the site are emergency situations, abusive relationships, children who witness, and teen dating violence, in addition to links to the warning signs of abuse, where to get help, and much more.

Paragraph 12 The research on dating violence and other forms of family violence is vast. Stets and Straus (1990) questioned the notion that the marriage license is a hitting license, if violent incidents occur in intimate relationships outside of marriage to the extent that they do. While researchers initially thought that violence between intimate others was confined to marriage, they now know this is not the case. In general, research on dating violence is studied as a distinct phenomenon, but is increasingly examined in the broader context of intimate violence.

REFERENCE LIST

Alabama Coalition Against Domestic Violence. (n.d.). Retrieved July 25, 2018, from http://www.acadv.org

Frieze, I. H. (2000). Violence in close relationships—development of a research area: Comment on Archer (2000). *Psychological Bulletin, 126*(5), 681-684.

Frieze, I. H. (2005). *Hurting the one you love: Violence in relationships.* Belmont, CA: Wadsworth.

Gelles, R. (1980). Violence in the family: A review of the research in the seventies. *Journal of Marriage and the Family, 43*(4), 878-885.

Google. (2018). Search: dating violence. Retrieved July 25, 2018, from http://www.google.com

Henton, J., Cate, R., Koval, J., Lloyd, S., & Christopher, F. (1983). Romance and violence in dating relationships. *Journal of Family Issues, 4*, 467-482.

Howard, D. E., & Wang, M. Q. (2003). Risk profiles of adolescent girls who were victims of dating violence. *Adolescence, 38*(149), 1-14.

James, W. H., West, C., Deters, K. E., & Armijo, E. (2000). Youth dating violence. *Adolescence, 35*(139), 455-465.

Laner, M. R., & Thompson, J. (1982). Abuse and aggression in courting couples. *Deviant Behavior, 3*, 228-244.

Letellier, P. (1994). Gay and bisexual male domestic violence victimization: Challenges to feminist theory and responses to violence. *Violence and Victims, 9*, 96-106.

Lobel, K. (Ed.). (1986). *Naming the violence: Speaking out about lesbian battering.* Seattle, WA: Seal Press.

Makepeace, J. M. (1981). Courtship violence among college students. *Family Relations, 30*(1), 97-101.

McKinney, K. (1986). Perceptions of courtship violence: Gender difference and involvement. *Free Inquiry into Creative Sociology, 14*, 55-60.

Pagelow, M. D. (1984). *Family violence.* New York: Praeger.

Renzetti, C. M. (1994). On dancing with a bear: Reflections on some of the current debates among domestic violence theorists. *Violence and Victims, 9*, 195-200.

Roscoe, B., & Benaske, N. (1985, July). Courtship violence experienced by abused wives: Similarities in patterns of abuse. *Family Relations, 34*(3), 419-424.

Steinmetz, S. K. (1977–1978). The battered husband syndrome. *Victimology, 2*, 499-509.

Stets, J. E., & Pirog-Good, M. A. (1989). Patterns of physical and sexual abuse for men and women in dating relationships: A descriptive analysis. *Journal of Family Violence, 4*(1), 67-76.

Stets, J. E., & Straus, M. A. (1990). The marriage license as a hitting license: A comparison of assaults in dating, cohabitating, and married couples. In M. A. Straus & R. J. Gelles (Eds.). *Physical violence in American families: Risk factors and adaptations to violence in 8,145 families* (pp. 227-244). New Brunswick, NJ: Transaction Books.

Straus, M. A., & Gelles, R. J. (1990). How violent are American families? Estimates from the national family violence resurvey and other studies. In M. A. Straus & R. J. Gelles (Eds.), *Physical violence in American families: Risk factors and adaptations to violence in 8,145 families* (pp. 95-112). New Brunswick, NJ: Transaction Books.

Appendix C

Worksheets

In this appendix you will find eleven worksheets that will guide you through the research and writing process. These are the worksheet numbers and their titles:

1. Selecting a Topic
2. Narrowing and Focusing Your Topic
3. Scholarly versus Popular Literature
4. Best Places for Information
5. Your Research Strategy
6. Locating Books
7. Chapters in Books
8. Locating Scholarly Articles
9. Evaluating Information
10. Outlining the Research Paper
11. Presentation

WORKSHEET 1
SELECTING A TOPIC

Name: _____ Date: _____

The purpose of this exercise is to brainstorm topics for which you are interested in writing your paper.

1. Write down three ideas you have for your paper. Select topics that are of interest to you, and meet the guidelines your professor has set for the course.

   Topic 1:

   Topic 2:

   Topic 3:

2. Select the *one* topic you are most interested in writing about. Why are you interested in exploring this topic?

3. What do you already know about this topic?

4. Using this topic, decide which discipline you will use in approaching the topic. For example, will you approach this topic from a sociological point of view, a psychological point of view, a criminal justice point of view?

5. From this topic, develop three possible research questions you might explore.

   Research Question 1:

   Research Question 2:

   Research Question 3:

WORKSHEET 2
NARROWING AND FOCUSING YOUR TOPIC

Name: _____ Date: _____

The purpose of this exercise is to develop a refined search question or statement.

1. What is the topic you wish to research (as you selected in Worksheet 1)?

2. What will be the time period of your research (e.g., last five years, last two decades, 1900s, comparing two decades [1970s and 2010s])?

3. What is the geographic area you are interested in exploring within this topic (e.g., United States, comparing two states [California and New York], a specific region [southeast], comparing two countries [Australia and Japan])?

4. What population or group will you be focusing on (e.g., men, women, children, adults, teenagers, the elderly, Irish, Scottish, African American, Hispanic)? Be as specific as possible.

5. What aspects or viewpoints will you focus on, as you determined in Worksheet 1 (sociological, economic, medical, etc.)? Remember, your research can be cross-disciplinary, meaning you can take more than one approach.

6. Taking the information from steps 1 through 5, write your topic in the form of a more refined research question or statement (e.g., What is the relationship between sex-role attitudes and work aspirations of adolescent girls and boys in the United States, comparing the 1970s to the 2010s?).

WORKSHEET 3
SCHOLARLY VERSUS POPULAR LITERATURE

Name: _____ Date: _____

The purpose of this exercise is to identify the differences between articles published in scholarly journals and those published in popular magazines. You can locate a scholarly journal and a popular magazine in one of two ways:

Step 1:

1. Go to the library and locate one issue of a scholarly journal and one issue of a popular magazine in print. Examples of scholarly journals are *American Journal of Sociology*, *Journal of the American Medical Association* (*JAMA*), and *Journal of Criminal Justice*. Examples of popular magazines are *People*, *Rolling Stone*, and *Time*.
2. Go to the library's website and locate the list of magazine and scholarly journal titles that the library subscribes to. Click on the link of a scholarly journal and a popular magazine, and then compare both publications online.

Step 2:

Using Table 2.1 in Chapter 2, compare the two publications and complete the following chart. You may select one article from each publication to answer the questions in the chart.

	Scholarly Journal	Popular Magazine
Title of Publication		
Date of Issue		
Advertisements Included?		
Length (in pages) of Article?		
Author(s) Given?		
Author(s) Credentials?		
References Given?		
Photographs Included?		
Other Differences:		

WORKSHEET 4
BEST PLACES FOR INFORMATION

Name: _____ Date: _____

The purpose of this exercise is to determine what kinds of information you need and to identify the best places to look for information on your topic.

A. Using your topic, check the kind of information you need for your research. Keep in mind course requirements (e.g., Does your professor want you to read scholarly articles as opposed to popular magazine articles?).

Your research question or statement:

Kind of Information Needed:

- Reference sources (reference books/e-books) (e.g., encyclopedias, dictionaries)
- Chapters in books
- Popular magazine articles
- Scholarly journal articles
- Websites
- Videos (documentaries)
- Interviews
- Statistics
- Other

B. Check the best places to look for the information you need. (Check all that apply.)

- Reference books in print—go to the library; Reference e-books—locate through the library's portal.
- Browse the library's book collection in selected LC Classification section(s) (e.g., BF, H, and R).
- Search the library's portal for online databases, online journals, video content, images, e-books, and other material.
- Search such search engines as Google Scholar.

WORKSHEET 5
YOUR RESEARCH STRATEGY

Name: _____ Date: _____

1. State your topic as completely as you can:

2. Circle two or three of the most important key words.

3. Write each key word you circled in step 2 in the space below, then list related terms (synonyms), if applicable.

                Key Word   Synonym

   a. _____   _____

   b. _____   _____

   c. _____   _____

   d. _____   _____

4. Write down any scholars' or experts' names on the topic that is being researched. If you do not know of any names, that is OK. Try checking your textbook or specialized encyclopedia on your topic for names of scholars who have researched your topic. You can then search for information about your topic by typing scholars' names into online databases and search engines.

You can now use the information on this worksheet to search various online and print resources for information on your research question.

WORKSHEET 6
LOCATING BOOKS

Name: _____ Date: _____

The purpose of this exercise is to locate two books on your chosen topic.

1. Search the library's online catalog/portal by subject or key word.

2. Locate two books on your topic. You can either locate a print version of the book in the library, or if it is an e-book, click on the link provided.

3. Write down the information for each book below.

Book 1

Author(s):

Title:

Date:

Place of publication (If more than one city is listed, select the city located closest to your home in the country in which you reside):

Publisher:

Call number (if a print book):

Book 2

Author(s):

Title:

Date:

Place of publication:

Publisher:

Call number (if a print book):

WORKSHEET 7
CHAPTERS IN BOOKS

Name: _____ Date: _____

The purpose of this worksheet is to enable you to obtain all information needed to correctly cite information taken from a chapter in a book, whether it is from a print book or an e-book. Select one book you have located on your topic. Then select the chapter out of the book and complete the worksheet.

Author(s) of the chapter:

Title of the chapter:

Date:

Editor(s) of the book (if the book is edited):

Title of the book:

Page numbers of the chapter:

Place of publication:

Publisher:

WORKSHEET 8
LOCATING SCHOLARLY ARTICLES

Name: _____ Date: _____

The purpose of this exercise is to locate two scholarly journal articles on your chosen topic. The articles can be in print or electronic format.

1. Search an online database through your library's portal or by searching Google Scholar. Search by subject, key word, or expert's name.

2. Locate two scholarly journal articles on your topic. Write down the information for each article below.

Article 1

Author(s):

Article title:

Journal title:

Issue date:

Volume number:

Issue number (if available):

Pages:

URL (if article is online):

Article 2

Author(s):

Article title:

Journal title:

Issue date:

Volume number:

Issue number (if available):

Pages:

URL (if article is online):

3. What online resource (e.g., online database, Google Scholar) did you search to locate these articles?

WORKSHEET 9
EVALUATING INFORMATION

Name: _____ Date: _____

Using the CRAAP test you learned about in Chapter 4, locate and evaluate an Internet site related to your topic.

1. What is your research question or statement?

2. What online resource did you search (e.g., Google, Yahoo)?

3. What subject(s), key words, and/or expert names did you search?

4. How many "hits" or "records" did you retrieve?

5. Locate a website related to your research topic and click on the link, then answer the following questions:

What is the Internet address? http:// (or https://) _____

What is the name of the website?

What is the purpose of the website?

What kind of information is included on the website? (Check all that apply.)
• Advertising
• Articles
• Graphics (images)
• Maps
• Statistics
• Video
• Other information

Who are the author(s) of the website?

What are the author(s) credentials (e.g., MD, PhD)?

What organization or institution are the author(s) affiliated with (college, university, institute, company, etc.)?

When was the website last updated?

How would this information be useful to you? If the information is not useful, why not?

WORKSHEET 10
OUTLINING THE RESEARCH PAPER

Name: _____ Date: _____

The purpose of this worksheet is to develop an outline for your research paper. You will then be able to use this worksheet to develop an organized research paper.

1. State your research question.

2. Complete this section of the worksheet by writing down three key points you will cover in your paper. Under each key point, write down three subpoints that support the main key point.

Key point 1 and subpoints to be addressed in paper:

    a.

    b.

    c.

Key point 2 and subpoints to be addressed in paper:

    a.

    b.

    c.

Key point 3 and subpoints to be addressed in paper:

    a.

    b.

    c.

3. Write down any notes that may be useful in completing your paper.

4. Write a draft of your concluding paragraph here.

5. List the references cited in your paper, using the appropriate style (e.g., APA style) here.

WORKSHEET 11
PRESENTATION

Name: _____ Date: _____

The purpose of this worksheet is to outline your presentation.

1. State your research question.

2. As you did in Worksheet 10, develop three key points and subpoints that you will cover in your presentation.

Key point 1 and subpoints to be addressed in presentation:

   a.

   b.

   c.

Key point 2 and subpoints to be addressed in presentation:

   a.

   b.

   c.

Key point 3 and subpoints to be addressed in presentation:

   a.

   b.

   c.

3. Write down any notes that may help you in your presentation.

4. Write a draft of your concluding paragraph for your presentation.

5. List references that you will be citing in your paper following a specific format, such as APA style. It is always a good idea to provide your audience with a list (paper or online) of the information you cited. In this way, the audience can read further on your topic.

6. Make a list of the technology (e.g., type of laptop, computer, software, microphone) that you will use in your presentation.

Appendix D

Blank Citation Forms

This appendix contains blank citation forms. Use the forms to record complete information about the sources you may cite in your paper. Forms contained in this appendix are for citing books, scholarly articles, chapters in books, and websites.

Whether you complete the forms in electronic or paper format, when you are done, place your resources in alphabetical order by the first author's last name to create your reference list (if you are using APA style). If no author appears for a citation, place that citation alphabetically by title. If there is more than one year listed, select the most recent. Please note that when citing the city of publication, select the city within your country that is closest to you geographically. For example, for a book with the following cities of publication listed: Toronto, Canada; New York; and San Francisco, California, if you are located in Buffalo, New York, you would list New York as the city of publication.

BOOK REFERENCES

Author(s):

Title of book:

Year of publication:

City of publication:

Publishing company:

Author(s):

Title of book:

Year of publication:

City of publication:

Publishing company:

Author(s):

Title of book:

Year of publication:

City of publication:

Publishing company:

Author(s):

Title of book:

Year of publication:

City of publication:

Publishing company:

CHAPTERS IN BOOKS REFERENCES

Author(s) of chapter:

Title of chapter:

Year of publication:

Editor(s) of book (if any):

Title of book:

Page numbers of chapter:

City of publication:

Publishing company:

Author(s) of chapter:

Title of chapter:

Year of publication:

Editor(s) of book (if any):

Title of book:

Page numbers of chapter:

City of publication:

Publishing company:

Author(s) of chapter:

Title of chapter:

Year of publication:

Editor(s) of book (if any):

Title of book:

Page numbers of chapter:

City of publication:

Publishing company:

JOURNAL ARTICLE REFERENCES

Author(s):

Title of article:

Year of publication:

Journal name:

Volume number:

Issue number (if available):

Page numbers of article:

URL (if journal is online):

Author(s):

Title of article:

Year of publication:

Journal name:

Volume number:

Issue number (if available):

Page numbers of article:

URL (if journal is online):

Author(s):

Title of article:

Year of publication:

Journal name:

Volume number:

Issue number (if available):

Page numbers of article:

URL (if journal is online):

INTERNET REFERENCES

Author(s) of article:

Name of article:

Date site/article was created:

Name of site (if different from article):

Author(s) of site (if different from article):

Date you accessed the site:

Name of online database (if applicable):

URL address:

Author(s) of article:

Name of article:

Date site/article was created:

Name of site (if different from article):

Author(s) of site (if different from article):

Date you accessed the site:

Name of online database (if applicable):

URL address:

Author(s) of article:

Name of article:

Date site/article was created:

Name of site (if different from article):

Author(s) of site (if different from article):

Date you accessed the site:

Name of online database (if applicable):

URL address:

Bibliography

Baumeister, R. F., & Vohs, K. D. (Eds.). (2007). *Encyclopedia of social psychology*. Los Angeles, CA: Sage.

Borgatta, E. F., & Montgomery, R. J. (Eds.). (2000). *Encyclopedia of sociology*. New York, NY: Macmillan.

Cook, K. N., Kunkel, L. R., & Weaver, S. M. (1995). Cooperative learning in bibliographic Instruction. *Research Strategies, 13*, 17-25.

Diagnostic and statistical manual of mental disorders: DSM-5, 5th edition (2013). Washington, DC: American Psychiatric Association.

Jackson, P. (2017). Bento box searching. *Public Libraries Online*. Retrieved from http://public librariesonline.org/2017/12/bento-box-searching/

Kuper, A., & Kuper, J. (Eds.). (2009). *The social science encyclopedia*. New York, NY: Routledge.

Maddox, G. L. (Ed.). (2001). *Encyclopedia of aging*. New York, NY: Springer.

Magill, F. N. (Ed.). (1994). *Survey of social science*. Englewood Cliffs, NJ: Salem Press.

Meehl, P. E. (1960). The cognitive activity of the clinician. *American Psychologist, 15*, 19-27.

PDR prescriber's digital reference. (2017). Whippany, NJ: ConnectiveRx. Retrieved from https://www.pdr.net/

Piotrowski, N. A. (Ed.). (2003). *International encyclopedia of social science: Psychology*. Hackensack, NJ: Salem Press.

Ponzetti, J. (Ed.). (2003). *International encyclopedia of marriage and the family*. New York, NY: Macmillan Reference USA.

Publication manual of the American Psychological Association, 6th edition. (2009). Washington, DC: APA.

Schulz, Richard. (Ed.). (2006). *Encyclopedia of aging*, 4th edition. New York, NY: Springer.

Sproull, N. L. (2002). *Handbook of research methods: A guide for practitioners and students in the social sciences*. Lanham, MD: Scarecrow Press.

Stearns, P. N. (Ed.). (2006). *Encyclopedia of social history*. New York, NY: Taylor & Francis.

Index

About the Author

Gail Staines is university librarian at the University of Central Missouri where she oversees the James C. Kirkpatrick Library and the Center for Teaching and Learning. She has held leadership positions at public and private universities as well as non-profit organizations, including serving as an executive director, board member, board vice president, and president. Her areas of research include information literacy, leadership, and library as place in academic environments. A successful grant writer for more than twenty years, Gail holds an MLS from the University at Buffalo as well as a PhD in higher education administration, also from the University at Buffalo.

CPSIA information can be obtained
at www.ICGtesting.com
Printed in the USA
LVHW111559010519
616260LV00009B/112/P

DATE DUE

APR 15 1975

OCT 2 3 1981

DEC 1 4 1981

NOV 1 0 1983

NOV 18 1987

APR 1 1990

MAY 0 7 1990